Life is what you make it!

by

Muriel & Pat Callis

Life is what you make it! Is dedicated to our Mother, who would have appreciated the title we chose, she had a hard life, but made the best of everything. We will always remain grateful to her for our Christian upbringing and her common sense and independence which she passed onto us.

To all our friends who have been mentioned in this book, including all the children who were members of our Youth group, without you the book, with its History, may never have been written.

First published in Great Britain in 2017 by RMC Media
RMC Media – www.rmcbooks.co.uk
6 Broadfield Court, Sheffield, S8 0XF
Tel: 0114 250 6300

Editor: Molly McGreevy
Design: Dan Wray

Printed and bound in Great Britain by CPI Colour Ltd.

A CIP catalogue record for this book is available from the British Library.

ISBN: 978-1-907998-28-7

Contents

With Mother

Part I

The 1930s

This is the true story of the life of two Sheffield sisters who commenced writing it in their eighties. We hope the readers will enjoy looking back to the 1930s onwards.

Muriel was born on St Valentine's Day - 14th February - 1929 at the Beauchief Nursing Home, Mother told us it was a cold winters day when the water in the pipes froze. Muriel's first home was at Tyzack Road, Woodseats. Her Baptism, which was normal practice, took place when she was about a month old at Sheffield Cathedral.

She would be two years old when the family moved to Gisborne Road, Ecclesall (the home they would live in until 1986) and where Pat was born on the 31st March 1932.

The Midwife Nurse Southard, lived in with the family for about a month. Apparently Father wanted to call Pat, "Olga", but this was changed to Patricia Mary when she was Baptised at Ecclesall All Saints Church on 1st May 1932.

Folk lore was still popular in the 1930s, one belief was that a baby born with a caul, a portion of membrane covering the baby's head, which has to be quickly removed to allow the baby to breath - was a good omen and charm against drowning. Sailors would pay good money to buy a caul. We were both born with a caul, the Matron at the nursing home kept Muriel's and Pat found hers in an envelope in a box many years later, and still has it.

Before Pat was born, Mother had the foresight to engage a young girl to help look after Muriel and it worked out very well. Her name was Florence, when Pat started talking she used to call her 'Florrie', her family were already known previously by both our parents, she was the eldest of four girls and was used to caring for them. Florrie was a lovely person, the salt of the earth, remaining a good friend to us all her life.

From a very early age we were encouraged to be thrifty. Soon after we were born, Father opened an account for us with the Trustee Savings Bank (TSB) and we became the proud owners of TSB money boxes.

These were metal boxes with a carrying handle, a slit for coins and a round hole to take ten shilling notes. When it was full it had to be taken to the bank to be unlocked and emptied. As we grew older it was a great excitement going to the bank and watching the coins drop out, the teller would count the money and put the amount in our bank book, then relock the box. It was a good way to learn that money doesn't grow on trees and if you wanted something badly, you had to save up for it and always live within your means.

The Gisborne Road house had a long garden, leading up to fields where the cattle from Haslam's Farm grazed. Soon after the fields were sold to build houses on Dobbin Hill, they also had long gardens, so we were not overlooked.

Father made a lovely garden with two lawns, rose beds, rose arches, apple trees and raspberry canes, a gentleman called Sinclair helped with the garden. We had Lombardy Poplar trees down part of one side and across the top of the garden, two Laburnum trees and two Prunus trees, which were all still blooming when we left Gisborne Road.

Father made a bird house near to the house so we could watch the birds going in and out from the dining room window. Our early years were idyllic, Muriel went to a dancing class run by Miss Robinson four houses up the road, and eventually we both went to Miss Cooper's dancing class at St William's Hall, Greystones.

Father was an Estate Agent and auctioneer, in his early days he used to keep horses in the Conisborough area, using a horse and trap to collect the

With Father

rents. Our first family holiday was in the late season of 1933, when we went to Blackpool to stay with our grand parents. Little did we know how our life was soon going to change.

In the spring of 1934 Father collapsed at the bottom of the stairs. He had suffered a stroke at 52-years-old, which left him with a degree of paralysis down his right side, he was cared for by Mother at home. Of course, all this was long before the health service and you had to pay the doctor for visiting. This happened when Muriel was starting school, which was very hard for her.

During the next four years Father suffered various degrees of strokes, although he was able to maintain a reasonable quality of life. Sinclair, who helped in the garden, used to have a game of cards with him, and father had a special wooden frame to put his cards on. We remember once, when Father went to the toilet, we took all the picture cards out of the pack, when he started looking at his cards, we had to own up, and we all had a good laugh.

Due to Father's illness we had to have a telephone, so he could keep in touch with his office. The telephone pole had to be put at the top of our garden, it was many years later, when more people wanted a telephone and we had several wires crossing the garden, that it was relocated to the grass verge of the road. In the early days, because of the war, there was always a shortage of lines and we had to have a party line, if you picked up the receiver and someone was speaking, you put it down quickly.

Father also liked to follow the horses and have a bet. On one occasion, when the horse called Jean's Dreams won the race, Father ordered a rocking horse from Redgates for the two of us.

In spite of his illness, Father insisted that we all had a holiday. We visited Morecambe, having a taxi to take us there, which was not as expensive as one would imagine. It was a large car which carried the five of us, Florrie came with us, and our luggage to the seaside on roads that were almost empty.

We stayed at a boarding house on the sea front and it was very flat, you could also hire tricycles. Pat had been put off eating dinners when she took a dislike to new potatoes, so at the boarding house all she had for dinner was a plate of raw carrots!

On one occasion we went on holiday by train, to Colwyn Bay, North Wales, and it was quite a job getting Father on to the train. We had a taxi to Victoria Station, which had to take us round to the luggage entrance in the Wicker and we all sailed up in the luggage lift.

Holiday at Blackpool

We had booked in at a boarding house, the landlady was very strict about being on time for meals! Also the accommodation was unsuitable. We noticed the Sunny Vale Holiday Camp at Kimnel Bay, near Rhyl, and decided to leave the boarding house and spend the rest of the holiday in a chalet there. It was an ideal holiday. There was lots for Father to watch, and things for the children to do and it was all flat.

Sometimes, when we were on school holidays and Father wasn't well, Florrie would take us to Blackpool and we stayed with the grandparents and

Florrie our lovely maid

Florrie would take us out. We would play at the amusement arcades and on the sands. On one occasion we were coming home on the train, and there were two elderly ladies, who treated us like royalty, as if we were princesses. At that age we did have similarities to Princesses Elizabeth and Margaret, and that is who they thought we were! Fortunately, this was sorted out quickly, much to the elderly ladies' embarrassment.

From an early age we attended Sunday School, which was held at Ecclesall Memorial Hall, Ringinglow Road, between 2:30pm and 3:30pm. We would sing songs and say simple prayers, then we would form a procession around the room and each gave a few pennies to the collection, which was kept in a wooden money box the shape of a church. We sang: "Hear the pennies dropping, listen how they fall, every one for Jesus, he shall have them all".

After this we would divide into groups of a similar age, for a story and expression work. Each week we were given a biblical stamp for our stamp books, through this we were taught about the church's year. On our birthdays we received a card, and everyone sang happy birthday. We also had concerts, for one concert Muriel was dressed as a snowdrop and Pat was a cornflower.

At Christmas we had a party and played lots of games, the popular ones included The Farmer's in his Den, In and Out the Windows and Orange and Lemons.

On Whit Sunday the girls wore white dresses and the boys had white shirts, a picture taken in our garden, showed us in white dresses with rosebuds, made by Mother. On Whit Monday there was a short church service and the traditional Whit Monday sing, followed by a procession to a field for games and a picnic.

In 1935 there were Jubilee Celebrations for the 25 years of King George V's reign; the school children received a small mirror to commemorate this event which Muriel still has.

Sadly, in January 1936 King George V died, and Edward VIII came to the throne, but before the year was out, due to personal reasons, the King abdicated in favour of his younger brother, the Duke of York. The Duke was proclaimed King George VI, his charming wife became Queen Elizabeth, and their two daughters Princess Elizabeth and Princess Margaret Rose.

On 12th May 1937, in spite of the unrest that could eventually end in war, the King's Coronation took place in Westminster Abbey amidst great celebrations. There was no television, but the newspapers produced the fantastic photographs, which we both recorded in scrap books. These scrapbooks have been passed on to two families with young children. The school children were given memorabilia in the form of scissors and spoons. We inherited several of these spoons from the neighbours,

Spring of 1937

12

Our Step Sister was married at Ecclesall Parish Church.
The reception was in our garden. Muriel and Pat were Bridesmaids.

which we had refurbished by one of Sheffield's Little Mesters, and remain in regular use today. We remember the Little Mesters, and the buffer girls, who polished the finished product, the girls worked very hard in dirty conditions.

In the same year as the Coronation, Olive, Father's daughter from his previous marriage, married George at Ecclesall All Saints Church. We were bridesmaids and Mother made pretty, long dresses, sashes and headbands for us to wear, and we carried small posies.

It was a lovely sunny day and we had lots of dainty goodies from Broughtons, a well-known shop near the Botanical Gardens and from a dairy called Maydews we had an enormous ice box of their homemade ice cream. Mother made the other refreshments. It was a very happy day.

To everyone's delight, in 1937 Muriel gained an Honours Certificate in ballet dancing, and Dad was so proud, a photograph was taken and framed to stand on the sideboard, where he could see it from his chair.

On 23rd January 1938 Father had another, severe stroke. We both went to Sunday school and Mother sent a note to Miss Slater, the Sunday School Superintendent, to say that Father was not expected to recover. A prayer was said in Sunday school and at Evensong in Church, the curate came and visited, but at 8pm that night, Father died.

Pat wanted to see Father and Olive took her upstairs to see him, but she was quite upset by it and for a long time she would not go upstairs on her own. The coffin was placed in the front room, remaining there until the funeral. The curate, Sam Price, came to the house to take the service before the burial at Tinsley Park Burial Ground, where Father's first wife was buried.

Muriel was very upset that we were not able to stay for the service, but our neighbours took us into their house. The house seemed full of people when everyone came back, Father's two sisters wanted to kiss us when they left, which we didn't like.

We still don't like being kissed on the mouth because Mother had a little boy, Jack, who had died when he was six-years-old from meningitis. Mother always instilled in us that this had been due to him drinking water from a communal cup in Endcliffe Park, and infection from kissing could do likewise. We always wore a Simpson's Iodine locket, to help protect us from infection.

It was at this time that Father's nephew, who took over father's business, visited us occasionally. He always wanted us to sit on his knee and we would run away from him. He was married with two children and was a practising chapel member and organist. It was strange, but we never felt safe with him as children. As we grew older we realised that we had been right to avoid him, he did cause a lot of problems.

After Father's death there was still a mortgage outstanding on the house, money was short, and Mother was ill with pleurisy and the menopause, she had heavy bleeding which sapped her energy. We had to pay for all medical care, and the doctor wanted her to go into hospital, but she wouldn't leave us.

Mrs Cullen, our neighbour, helped with food, washing and making the beds. When Mother started to improve, Aunt Carrie paid for us to have a holiday at the Sunnyvale Holiday Camp and she came with us.

We both attended Ecclesall C of E Primary School, Ringinglow Road, which was about 15 minutes from home. To get to school we had to cross a busy road, but there was always a policeman to see us across safely.

Our Great Aunt took us away to Sunny Vale Camp 1937

In those days you would be given a certificate at the end of each term if you had attended school every day and had never been late. We were very proud of these, which were signed by Mr Newton, Chief Education Officer, and Mr Jenkinson, our Head Teacher. We were lucky not to take time off school, as the only infections we had –measles and chickenpox – occurred in the school holidays.

As a church school we had a Christian assembly every morning immediately after the registers had been taken. We had hymns and prayers and a thought for the day and on special Holy days, such as Ash Wednesday and Good Friday, all the school walked to the church for a special service, the rest of the day was a holiday.

We continued to go to dancing class and gained certificates in December 1938. Muriel was just six points short of another honours certificate, and Pat also passed, although she had problems when finishing one of the dances, she had her back to the judges!

The war years

On 3rd September 1939 life was turned upside down.

Dancing classes stopped, but the children held concerts, to help the war effort. It was announced that there would be a National Registration Day on 29th September 1939, every household had to fill in a form giving details who lived there. By the end of the year, everyone had been issued with an identity card, our number was KKCG 170/ 1 for Mother, /2 for Muriel and /3 for Pat. This was quickly followed by gas masks being issued, these were in square cardboard boxes and it was up to the owners to provide carrying straps, there were special ones for babies and very young children. We had to carry them everywhere, and in school we sometimes wore our gas mask for lessons, to familiarise ourselves with them.

Then we had to have an Anderson air raid shelter in the garden, a large area had to be excavated to quite a depth, the shelter was fixed into the cavity then it had to be covered with soil and sandbags. There was a front entrance and an emergency exit at the back, in order to get out we had to position a stepladder on the outside at the rear, to climb out. This was in case the main entrance was blocked with debris.

In front of the main door we had to build a thick blast wall with bricks and concrete, as far as we can remember the wall had to be at least four bricks in depth, we all had to build this with the help of friends and neighbours. We children were quite expert at mixing cement, which all had to be mixed with shovels by hand.

All the houses had to have brown paper strips stuck on the windows, so that the glass wouldn't be shattered by the blast from the bombs and

At the rear exit of the Air Raid Shelter

the guns. Blackout material had to be bought to line all the curtains, so that no light could be seen. Each road had wardens and they would walk round at night, and shout, 'put that light out' if anyone had a light showing. The wardens were provided with tin helmets to wear when they were patrolling. Our two main wardens were Mr Shepherd and Mr Burden and they watched us very well. Not everyone had a shelter, if you lived in a house with a cellar, the cellar was re-enforced to make it suitable for a shelter. The church had a crypt which was used as a shelter for the senior children, who had their lessons in one of the Memorial Rooms. The Crypt was also used by the public.

Inside the shelter, were bunks to sleep on and paraffin lamps to give light. You had to be sure the wick was trimmed and you had a box of matches. We also kept some emergency rations in a tin box, sealed with adhesive tape. Should we be in bed when the sirens sounded, to get out quickly we had siren suits, they were very warm and had buttons at the

OPERATIC SECTION.
THE ROYAL ACADEMY OF DANCING
Incorporated by Royal Charter
(Formerly
The Association of Operatic Dancing of Great Britain.)

CHILDREN'S EXAMINATIONS

Grade **I**

MARKS.

Technique	Arms	Adage	Steps	Dances	Mime	Theory	Total
20	10	20	20	20	5	5	100
18	9	17	15	17	4	5	85

Result—
Honours 85
Passed 65

REMARKS *Excellent work. Retirés require practice, + knees should be easier in Jetés.*

Examiner *Olive Handley.*

Muriel (*above*) and Pat's (*below*) dancing certificates from 1937 and 1938

OPERATIC SECTION.
THE ROYAL ACADEMY OF DANCING
Incorporated by Royal Charter
(Formerly
The Association of Operatic Dancing of Great Britain)

CHILDREN'S EXAMINATIONS

Grade **I**

MARKS.

Technique	Arms	Adage	Steps	Dances	Mime	Theory	Total
20	10	20	20	20	5	5	100
15	7	13	14	13	4	4	70

Result— *Pass*
Honours 85
Passed 65

REMARKS *Battements tendus vague. Chassés forgotten. Pirés + jetés good. Mime should be done facing examiner.*

Examiner *Theresa Heyman*

back which you undid to go to the toilet or rather use the bucket, if you were in the shelter.

On the first night of the War, 3rd September, the air raid sirens sounded and we all went out to the shelters. Our shelter had not yet been completed, so we joined our neighbours next door, who had made a shelter from their coal house, covering it with sand bags and soil, with a blast wall in front of the entrance. After a short time the 'all clear' sounded and we all trooped back home.

It was a good job it was a phoney siren, because we had not had time to complete all the preparations for war, but at least it gave us an idea of what to expect.

The schools had to start building air raid shelters and Ecclesall School was closed for several terms, in the interim period, home service lessons were provided. Our next door neighbours above were both teachers at Greystones School, and they had classes in their house. Our wooden clothes horse was loaned to them with hooks screwed in, for the children to hang their coats. Muriel and Pat went there, the younger ones in the morning and the older ones in the afternoon, we also had homework to do.

After a short time Greystones School was re-opened and as it was nearer for us, we went there until Ecclesall School re-opened. Many of the children had a father who was fighting in the war, and one day a pile of beautiful dolls arrived at the school to be given to those children, there were two dolls left over and they were given to us, as we didn't have a father.

We must have been at least one term at Greystones School, then we returned to Ecclesall School. This was very disruptive, particularly for those taking their 11+ exam, which Muriel was, and unfortunately she did not pass.

During the war, High Storrs Grammar School was used as a refuge centre and for emergency accommodation, providing food and clothing for the homeless. There was a Big Bertha gun and barage balloons on their playing fields. There were also barrage balloons on the tennis courts near the Botanical Gardens. The Blue Coat School on Psalter Lane was evacuated and it was taken over by the army and its vehicles. On the moors they used lights as decoys, to encourage the German planes to drop the bombs there rather, than in the city.

During the war there was a shortage of lodgings and we were all encouraged to take boarders, which also helped a little financially. We had one long term boarder, Mr Riley, who had the box room, he was deputy manager in the National Westminster Bank. He used to call Pat Shrimpey, and each morning he had a pinch of snuff, he always used to offer us a pinch, which made us sneeze.

Mr Parks also spent some time living with us, he was a teacher and his fiancée, a maid called Bella, lived with relatives of our neighbours. Mr Parks used to take us walking in Derbyshire, until he was later conscripted. Then we had a Mr Quarrie, from London, who had a senior job at Balfour's steel works, the firm provided Adexolin vitamin tablets for all their workers, to keep them fit and reduce sick leave. Mr Quarrie's wife, later joined him when they had found a suitable house, she became an English teacher at Abbeydale Grammar School. Lastly Mr Wharton lodged with us. He worked for Kelly's Directory, which brought him to Sheffield from time to time.

If there were more than two visitors at the same time ourselves and Mother had to sleep in the front room downstairs, between the settee and easy chairs, or on the floor. In the morning, we had to be up early to put the room to rights before the boarders got up. We became very good at preparing and serving breakfast.

Ration Books were issued in January 1940. As children we were allowed extra milk, our grandparents were always short of tea and we were always short of butter, so we did an occasional switch, to this day we do not drink tea.

To make the butter go further we had a two-pound jam jar and someone designed a churn to fit over the jar and we put milk in with the butter, turned the handle until it was it was well mixed, and it made double of the original amount. Later on margarine was produced, but it wasn't very palatable. We also had to get used to national bread, which was a mixture of coarse brown flour.

The Wedding! At Sheffield Cathedral of Dr. Jack Hopewell and Joan Whittaker at the beginning of the War with eight bridesmaids including Muriel and Pat

Everyone was told to dig for victory, so apart from a grass edging to walk on, the lawn was dug up and we attempted, not always very successfully, to grow vegetables, particularly potatoes.

In the early part of the war, our cousin, Dr Jack Hopewell, married Joan Whittaker, a dancing teacher, in Sheffield Cathedral. We were asked to be bridesmaids alongside six of Joan's friends. Fortunately, we didn't have to provide our dresses, and regardless of the limited clothing coupons, we were fitted out with beautiful long gowns. Joan wanted us to carry white prayer books, as flowers were in short supply. There was only one shop where she was able to purchase the books, it wasn't until after the wedding that we saw they were Roman Catholic books.

Although it was a dull day, we remember crowds watching the procession, after all it was unusual to have eight bridesmaids, particularly in war time! Jack had been called up into the Army Medical Corps, and had been posted to Bridgewater in Somerset.

There were a few air raids during this period of the war, but nothing of note until December 1940. On Saturday 7th December, Mother told us that she would have to pawn a diamond ring, in order to raise some money for food. We went into a Jewellers on Devonshire Street, Sheffield, where the owner of the shop examined the ring with his eye glass. He told us there was a flaw in the ring and he could only give us £5. Mother pondered this but we needed the money, and she thought she would be able to recover the ring at some stage, so she accepted the money.

On the way home, we stopped at the Sheffield & Ecclesall Co-operative Store at the bottom of the Moor for a cheap, nourishing meal of liver and onions. At that time we only had one boarder, Mr. Riley, and he paid 25 shillings a week for bed, breakfast and an evening meal.

The evening of Thursday 12th December was a beautiful night, with a full moon and a crisp frost, making visibility good. Attercliffe, including five miles of steel works alongside the River Don was enveloped in a protective blanket of thick ground fog.

Muriel was practising for a concert which was to take place the following evening, wearing the long Cinderella dress she was to wear when she was dancing with Prince Charming on Friday, when the sirens sounded at 6:45pm.

Before we could get to the air raid shelter, planes were overhead, the Big Bertha Gun making everything shake. We felt helpless, what could we do? Mother decided we should turn the dining room table on its side against the window in case the glass was shattered. We sat under the table, drinking a bottle of ginger wine that had been bought for Christmas from the Rington's Tea man that day.

The noise was horrendous, the wardens could be heard stamping out the incendiary fire bombs. When there was a lull outside, they shouted through the letter box, asking if we were alright. During one apparent lull Mother gently opened the front door only to be sent flying by a blast. It was frightening, we could hear the drone of planes coming over wave after wave. The fire bombs formed a circle, guiding the planes for dropping the high explosives.

All we could do was huddle together, keep warm and wait. The Blitz lasted nine hours and it wasn't until 4:15am the next morning that the all-clear sounded. We looked out over Sheffield from the front bedroom window to see The Moor, the main shopping road, was on fire from one end to the other. Exhausted, we tried to get some sleep.

The telephones were not working, so we could not contact our great aunt, who lived at Millhouses, where the railway ran at the bottom of her garden, making her home a vulnerable target. Mother said we must go down to see if she was safe.

With no transport available we started walking. There were lumps of shrapnel on the roads, and the nearer we got to Millhouses, the more damage we saw.

Abbeydale Grammar School had been hit and was badly damaged, a house at the corner of Archer Lane was completely demolished and the majority of houses we passed had broken windows and other damage. Panic was with us as we walked along the road to where Aunt Carrie lived, every window was broken. When we arrived at her house, there was no sign of her. Mother shouted her name and she came up from the cellar unharmed. The broken windows were quickly boarded up, eventually to be replaced with special unbreakable glass.

We had not had any communication with our lodger Mr Riley and knew he was working at a bank in Millhouses, which had been demolished following a direct hit. It was three days before we found that he was safe, he had apparently gone into Sheffield and when the sirens went, took refuge in the library shelter and had been giving out tots of whisky to all and sundry. He walked up Ecclesall Road to get home, and told us what a lot of damage there was; he had seen an army of rats wending their way to the suburbs.

Our neighbours had been taken to stay with their relatives in a large detached house, at the top of Bingham Park, their large cellar had been reinforced. They had an unexploded bomb in their garden which had to be dealt with by the bomb disposal squads. They were told if it had been a few yards nearer and exploded, they could have all been killed.

The damage in Sheffield was horrendous and it included the Jewellers shop on Devonshire Street, so mother was never able to recover her pawned ring. The next three days we were blessed with fine weather. By Sunday, in the town centre, the clearing of the horrendous mess continued. There were happy meetings when friends and relatives were reunited alongside grief, horror and numbness at the sight of large areas of Sheffield, our city, reduced to rubble.

Buses started to run, but the trams had taken a battering, the tracks and overhead lines required repairing but everyone was settling down and getting on with life, regardless. There were services held in many churches, on the Sunday afternoon The Messiah was sung in the Victoria Hall in front of an audience of more than 200 people, just as it had been sung for years, prior to Christmas. The Hall was a large building in the centre of Sheffield, it was amazing it had not been damaged.

On the afternoon of Sunday 15th December there was the first daylight alert of the war, which suggested the presence of a reconnaissance plane.

At 6:50pm, the sirens sounded, this time the planes came from the north east to the segment of the city that had been almost untouched on the previous raid. The bombing was intensive until the all clear sounded at 10:17pm. The bombs had been of particularly high calibre and included fourteen parachute mines. Two of the mines didn't explode, but the others caused terrible damage in the Firth Park, Darnall, Attercliffe, Tinsley and Brightside areas. There was no attack beyond Tinsley.

We were anxious to find out if Florence and her family, who lived on Weedon Street, Carbook, were safe. Florence had stopped being our maid when Father died, but her family were still our good friends. They had a small grocery and general household shop opposite to the steelworks. Many of the men in the steelworks were called up, to be replaced by women and young girls making munitions, including Florence and her sisters, it was hard, dirty work.

We had a very tortuous journey to Tinsley and it was such a relief to see the shop and the family intact, albeit in a state shock following the bombardment.

The Nazis had completed their circle of the proud city of Sheffield, reducing much of it to rubble and killing nearly 2,000 civilians and servicemen in just over 12 hours of deadly conflict. But what Hitler didn't know was that "Sheffielders were a tough, resilient race".

Pat with her class in Ecclesall School playground

The aftermath

After the two horrendous raids, Hitler must have realised that there wasn't much left to bomb, because the raids became infrequent. When the workers had cleared some of the rubble in the centre, one or two shops were opening, and we could take a bus down to the bottom of Ecclesall Road, this is what we saw.

The large Sheffield and Ecclesall Co-operative was virtually undamaged, apart from windows that had been blown out and had been quickly replaced. All their departments were open: the grocery, shoes, clothing and the restaurant. Across the road there was a shoe shop still standing, but when we turned the corner to walk up the Moor towards the virtually unscathed Town Hall we found Atkinsons, Robert Brothers, Redgates, Central Picture Palace, Marks and Spencers, Williams Trimming House, British Home Stores, the Empire Theatre had been almost razed to the ground.

Into Fargate, the second Marks and Spencers, Arthur Davy, the coffee shop and grocery, Proctors and Cole Brothers were all badly damaged. Walsh's was flattened, and until it could be rebuilt, they opened their store at The Mount, Broomhill, a very large house with grounds. This had to be used for many years, until rebuilding was completed.

Continuing our journey down Angel Street, Cockayne's, C&A, Symington Crofts, and the Brightside and Carbrook Co-perative were all badly damaged. Amazingly, the Market Hall on Dixon Lane, was still there. In Fitzalan Square the large Marples Hotel had received a direct hit. The hotel, which had an extensive network of cellars, was full of customers on the night of the Blitz, and had the largest number of fatalities in one building, more than 70 people were killed there, and only seven survived.

Looking at Sheffield now, it is hard to believe how it was restored: first by erecting pre-fabricated buildings, then gradually rebuilding. Unfortunately, many of the businesses fell by the wayside.

Following the raids, the water supply was seriously disrupted due to damaged pipes, we had to carry every available container to get water from the mobile water carts. Not one drop of water could be wasted and after we had used a small amount of water for washing it would be taken to the bathroom for flushing the toilet. The local authority worked hard to get the facilities back to normality, so that life could be resumed in a productive manner.

Our Mother applied and was accepted for a Night Supervisors post and factory nurse, as she had a first aid certificate for £4-10 shillings a week. The firm was Frank Guylees, a small tools firm on Archer Road, Millhouses. Then she worked nights, so that she was able to be look after us during the day, and had to walk through the dark streets to get to her 12-hour shift. During the night we were often cared for by our Aunt Carrie, and an elderly lady from church helped out occasionally.

They were quite a mixed group at the factory, men and women, leading to a lot of bad language, Mother organised a swear box and anyone caught swearing had to put money in the box. The money raised, which was quite considerable, was taken to the Wolfenden Rehabilitation Centre, Fulwood, where injured soldiers were sent to recuperate.

After about a year, Mother had to leave, the long hours were affecting her health and the tax people wanting their share made it impossible to make ends meet.

As we mentioned at the start of the war we held concerts to raise money for various war efforts. This included Whist Drives and these were very popular, they were held during the day as it was difficult going out at night with the blackout restrictions.

But we both continued to support the Merchant Navy Comforts Fund, by making lavender and moth ball bags, which we put on a wooden tray

Concerts in the garden in aid of the Merchant Navy

and sold to all the residents in the area. We also had concerts, either in our own or our neighbours' gardens. We still have the letters, and a book that was written by Kirkland Bridge who organised parcels for the Merchant Navy Comfort Fund. Without them risking their lives to bring us food, the country would have been in a bad state.

A lady whom Mother had worked with had given her an address of a Mrs Mainprize, who lived at Reighton, near Filey, and took guests in for a weeks holiday. It was a farm cottage with a small holding, they had free range chickens, a couple of pigs, a few cows and they grew their own vegetables. We had a marvellous week living off the fat of the land and although we cannot remember what she charged, it was very little. From the dining room you could see the sea and watch the convoys steaming across the bay. The mined sands were out of bounds and barbed wire prevented people going down and anyone landing. All the sign posts in the country had been obliterated, because of the fear of invasion. We enjoyed it so much that we went again the following year, taking our ex-maid Florence, giving her a much needed break.

We were both confirmed at the age of 13 years, for which we were carefully prepared for by the Vicar and Curates at All Saints Church, Ecclesall. This was a big event in our lives.

Muriel was confirmed at St. Andrew's, Sharrow, on 15th March 1942, due to illness Mother was unable to attend her confirmation, so we walked over two miles to the church just the two of us. Muriel wore a white dress with long sleeves and a white veil. There were only four or five children from Ecclesall Church confirmed with Muriel, as the churches took it in turn to hold the confirmation service.

Pat was confirmed on 11th March 1945 at Ecclesall Church wearing the dress that Muriel had worn, the white veils were provided by the church. More than 30 boys and girls were confirmed, several wore their Guide uniform, rather than a white dress, due to clothes rationing. Mother, Muriel and Aunt Carrie went to the service. We were given special communion prayer books, which we both still have.

Sheffield's final air raid was on 17th July 1942, but we still had to carry our gas masks and identity cards, in case there were further raids. Rationing continued for food, sweets and clothing until well after the end of the war.

In 1943, it was Pat's turn to sit the scholarship exam, Pat was successful in the examination and gained a place in her first choice, Abbeydale Grammar School for Girls. Pat had to have the appropriate school uniform, which we had to ensure would last as long as possible, as clothing was scarce. We also had to buy books and on the first day of the September term, all the pupils had to make a cover for each of their six to eight books, but this was the only time we had to pay for books. We were spoilt in the first year, by a delightful headmistress, called Miss Mullen, she used to have us in groups in her office, to get to know us all.

Unfortunately, she left Sheffield the following year. The school was a building site for most of Pat's school days due to the damage caused by the Blitz. Sadly, the gym was not rebuilt for use until 1947, and when Pat left school in 1948 there were still areas to be completed.

Muriel had reached a stale mate with her education and most of her time was spent helping one of her class mates with maths. During her last few months,

Muriel was given the opportunity to attend art college one afternoon a week. Six girls from different schools had been recommended by their teachers to join the class and showed aptitude for further training. Muriel found learning the different techniques very interesting, particularly nature studies, scenery, animals and free hand drawing, which was more difficult. The knowledge she gained came in useful in later years, especially when she became a Sunday school teacher.

During this period, Mother worked part-time nights as a nursing assistant at Nether Edge Hospital. She was also asked to do private night sitter jobs.

Mother continued to work long hours to give Muriel the opportunity to attend Whitely's Business Training College full-time, but this required her to leave traditional education three months earlier than normal. On the advice of Mr Jenkinson, Headmaster at Ecclesall School, Mother wrote to the Chief Education Officer requesting permission for her to transfer to the college, this was granted.

Whitely's was a private long established college, undertaking courses in Pitman shorthand, typing, accounts, tots, handwriting and spelling. There were several different tutors and teaching was sometimes in groups or individually. Muriel was so grateful that Mother gave her this chance to learn this basic knowledge, which held her in good stead in the years to come.

Muriel spent three terms at Whitely's, travelling daily to the centre of Sheffield. She was issued with a card and badge which enabled her to pay half price on the trams. She loved the maths section, how to present accounts, income and expenditure, balance sheets, typing and shorthand, which was the most difficult. In July 1943, her first report stated that her handwriting was improving, shorthand was fairly good, book keeping was progressing well and typing, maths, business methods and correspondence were all good. Mother never said how much it cost to go there and we were always anxious to start earning a wage to help the family budget, we had a Saturday morning job delivering meat which earned us each two shillings and six pence.

The local newspapers were scanned to find something suitable for Muriel and eventually the following advert was seen: Junior office girl required in the Broomhill area.

Along with a few more she was asked to go for interview, it was an Employers' Association. A few days before the interview we went to find the building, it was a very large house in grounds and was within 30 minutes walking distance of our home. Following the interview Muriel was delighted to be offered the position at £1- 5 shillings a week. After the first month all the staff received a one-off bonus and Muriel's was two shillings extra, which Mother said she must buy something for herself and she bought a scarf from Marks and Spencer. £1 was given to the family budget and five shillings spending money to provide clothing and shoes, anything left over went in her money box.

Muriel spent 18 months at Sheffield Lighter Trades Employers' Association, learning good procedures. At first I was in the general office, which was a large room in the attic along with the typists' pool. My main jobs were making tea and coffee, filing and learning to use the copying machine and addressograph.

I was soon asked to learn switchboard work, so I could take over at lunch times. When the next new junior arrived, I was transferred to the ground floor reception area, where I received visitors and operated the telephone switchboard. It was enjoyable being on the reception desk, seeing and greeting members of the association, who arrived for meetings in the large conference room. The envelopes I had helped to address came alive when I asked their names, and I soon began to recognise their voices on the telephone when answering their calls. It was another big learning curve in memory training, I can still remember the telephone number of Lighter Trades House. Although I was very happy there, I wanted to expand my knowledge by having a career. I would have liked to have join one of the services, but was not old enough.

Staff at Lighter Trades Employers' Association

31

Growing up

Pat - a proud Brownie

Pat had joined the Brownies when she was 10-years-old, which was late, so she was only a Brownie for less than a year before transferring to the Girl Guides. Uniforms were passed down from one to another, due to cost and clothing coupons.

The 65th Ecclesall Guides met on a Friday evening and for six years Pat was an enthusiastic Guide, from her initial enrolment ceremony to obtaining over a dozen badges in different subjects and becoming a First Class Guide.

The first guide camp I attended was in 1943 at Hathersage, where the tents had to be camouflaged because of the war. We had to take a trek-cart filled with tents, equipment and our kitbags down to the station for the short journey to Hathersage. A trek cart needs one person on the central pole guiding it, then at each corner of the cart a rope

Pulling the trek cart

is attached with a person on each rope. When you went up hill those on the ropes pulled from the front, when going downhill, you pulled from the back, to prevent the cart from running away.

The tents were erected in a field high on the hill. It was quite a hard journey with the trek-cart climbing the hill. There were probably about 20 guides camping and we had a great time. We went on lots of walks, visited the outdoor swimming pool, and I remember one evening walking over to Eyam, where there was a small fairground, which we all enjoyed. From what I can remember we were able to get most of our food locally, and we took the trek cart down into the village three or four times during the week.

On the last evening we had a camp fire singing all the camp songs and the following year we camped at Hathersage again.

It is always said that school days are the happiest days, but Pat would not agree. At Grammar school I enjoyed the domestic science and sports but maths and science were always a bit of a mystery.

During my schooldays, one of our class was not very clean and we were asked to help and befriend her. Unfortunately, many of the class had to be treated for head lice and I was one of the unfortunate ones. It was a weekend when Mother found that I had been infected and in that two days I must have had my hair washed and combed with a nit comb a dozen times. Come Monday morning at school, the 'nit nurse' came to inspect the whole class, and I was passed as clear! It was a shame that the culprit wasn't seen after this, after all she had passed the scholarship to come to the school, and she and her family needed help.

When I was in about the third or fourth year a new history mistress came, who brought a lot of interest to the subject. We also had a new English mistress, who showed empathy, encouraging us all to do well. The teachers had and still have a great responsibility to their pupils.

Meanwhile, Muriel, who so far had never wanted to join a youth group, but had always been interested in helping people, decided to join the St. John Ambulance Brigade, following in Mother's footsteps. The local division met in the church hall on Wednesday evenings, so Muriel went along every week and eventually was confident to take and pass the first aid and home nursing exams. Little did any of us realise that this would be the start of bigger things.

On 8th May 1945 we were celebrating Victory in Europe, we listened to the radio, hardly able to believe that part of the war was over. In many areas there were street parties, dancing in the street, everyone entering in to the excitement. But the celebrations soon faded, as there were still so many post war problems.

This was followed a year later by Victory in Japan. This had been a terrible war, our soldiers were taken prisoner by the Japanese, cruelly treated and made to work on the Burma Road. Many soldiers died and those who survived were in a terrible state. To end this war, the Americans used atom bombs, the deadliest of weapons, causing horrendous damage, loss of many lives and many long term problems, such as radiation. It was a great shock to everyone that these had been used.

1946

Muriel started to look for a change. I did tell my employers that I was on the lookout for something different. The firm was sorry that I would be leaving and they asked if I had a friend that might be interested in Switchboard work. A good friend from school days sprang to mind and she jumped at the opportunity. Freda worked there for many years.

I had been looking in The Star adverts for a few weeks when I found an advert for a dental receptionist, experience not necessary. I had no idea what it would entail, but I applied and at the interview I was asked if I fainted at the sight of blood. I was accepted to start work the first week of June 1946.

The practice was on Alderson Road, off London Road, the names on the door were Mr McGhee and Mr Reeve, I never met Mr Reeve because he was away in the army and Mr McGhee was an MP and worked in the surgery part time – two days in Sheffield and one day at the branch practice in Chesterfield, the rest of the time he was in London.

I will never forget that first Monday, we had four patients booked in to have all their teeth out, with a local doctor giving the open ether anaesthetic, this was administered on to a gauze mask over the nose and mouth. It all seemed very crude at first, but it was a very normal method 70 years ago. They certainly knew how to operate, being a quick and efficient team, it was soon over.

My main job was looking after the patients in the recovery room, then when they ready to go home, I had to do all the clearing up. This included washing all the sponges used to remove all traces of blood. There were no plastic gloves for me to wear, I soaked them in Dettol, rinsed and dried them ready for the next session.

When the dentist was not working, I thoroughly cleaned the surgeries, made appointments and filled in the claim forms patients brought in from different insurance firms, this was before the National Health Service started. I enjoyed the work but did not like being on my own when I had to travel to Chesterfield to clean one day a week. When the dentist was working I was taken by car, otherwise I had to go by bus.

I was still on my starting wage of £1-5 shillings, but on my first pay day, I was 5 shillings short, Mrs McGhee who did the wages thought my wage was £1, but she gave me the extra 5 shillings. It was not a good start, so I had to learn as much as I could and start looking for a new post, determined not to be out of work.

Fortunately, it was not too long before I found an advert for a trainee dental receptionist, I applied for the post, and at the interview I was offered a starting salary of £1-5 shillings per week. I worked at the Alderson Practice for four months and on 1st October 1946 I started working with Mr Fyffe, on City Road, who was to be my employer for the next 20 years.

Pat was still at school and on the 8th June 1946 a message was sent to all school children from King George Vl in the form of a card, with the King's Coat of Arms, that you could hang up. This was the King's message:

"Today, as we celebrate Victory, I send this personal message to you and all other boys and girls at school. For you have shared in the hardships and dangers of total war and you have shared no less in the triumph of the Allied Nations. I know you will always feel proud to belong to a country which was capable of such supreme effort; proud, too, of parents and elder brothers and sisters who by their courage, endurance and enterprise brought victory. May these qualities be yours as you grow up and join the common effort to establish among the nations of the world unity and peace."

On the reverse side was a list of the important war dates, including the first atomic bomb that was dropped on Hiroshima 6th August 1945, the second atomic bomb was dropped on Nagaski 9th August 1945.

Feeding the pigeons in Trafalgar Square

In 1946, those girl guides who had become First Class Guides were invited to London to the first International Guide Rally, where the two Princesses were going to take the salute at a march past on the Mall.

As far as I can remember we didn't have to pay for this, apart from a little spending money. Prior to going we had to attend marching practice, undertaken by a soldier at Somme Barracks, Sheffield. He prepared us for the long parade which would start at Horse Guards Parade, follow the length of the Mall and beyond Buckingham Palace. We were instructed how to perform eyes right upon command as we were about to pass the Princesses. Finally, we were told to look smart and use spit and polish on our shoes.

We caught an early train to London on the Saturday; it was a lovely fine, warm day. When we arrived in London we made our way to Trafalgar Square, where we had a picture taken feeding the pigeons. We did an amazing amount of sightseeing, eventually arriving at the Camden Town deep underground shelter, where we stayed overnight, sleeping on the bunks, not that we slept for long, with the excitement and the noise of the trains above passing through the tube station.

On the Sunday we made our way to Buckingham Palace where we were able to go into the Royal Mews and were shown the royal cars, coaches and beautiful horses. We must have had something to eat but what stuck in my mind was a fizzy drink, and a scoop of ice cream, which was delicious.

We made our way to Horse Guards Parade with hundreds of other girl guides, where we were put into long columns. It was a boiling hot day and the first aiders were kept busy resuscitating those who fainted. The band struck up and the parade started, the Princesses were on a platform about half way along the Mall, and we all listened carefully for the eyes right command as we passed close to them. Then the magical moment was over and we continued parading until we were given the command to 'Halt and Fall Out.' Then a very tired, but happy, group made our way to the train to come home.

When Pat was preparing for the International Rally, Mother and Muriel both helped to make sure that she looked smart, but the one item of clothing which let her down was her Gabardine raincoat, which had been purchased from a pawn shop a few months previously, and had started to rot. Pat repaired and carefully pressed it, but we did not have the money to buy a new one.

A few days after Pat came back from London, Mother was visited by our Vicar, Canon Jordan, who said that he understood that she had financial problems. Mother said that it was difficult, but we were managing. He then insisted that he wanted to give her £8, just to help us out. Someone well known to us must have spoken to the vicar, but we had no idea who it was.

So Pat had a new raincoat and proudly wore it at the next guide meeting, only to be greeted by Captain, who said: "Oh Pat, why couldn't you have had it when we went to London?"

Pat was upset because she knew how hard Mother worked to keep the house and family going. It was also an object lesson, as you never know a family's situation.

Muriel and Pat both decided that they would repay the gift in some way and we hope that anyone who reads our story will realise how we have endeavoured to do just that.

Mother impressed on us we must always work and we should have a career. This kindness was a turning point for our family and Mother never forgot it. She asked us that when she died, she would like her ashes buried in sight of Canon Jordan's grave in Ecclesall Church Yard, we were able to fulfil her wish.

Following the excitement of VE day and VJ Day, Pat found it very upsetting when we had to go into the School Hall and listen to people who came to lecture us in school, about how the future was going to be affected after the war and particularly with the use of the Atom Bombs, and the danger we could all be in, at any time. I found it very upsetting and was petrified with what they were saying, and tried to close my ears to it.

Thankfully I was able to talk it through with mother and she reassured me. I never found out how the rest of the school had reacted to this bombardment, it was just something I wanted to forget. I felt it was totally unnecessary at that time, when we were preparing for exams.

Needless to say, there was a lot of unrest in the world and in England there were groups forming Ban the Bomb Marches and Peace Marches. One protest which lasted years was organised by women at Greenham Common.

1947

During the war years there were many stray dogs and large numbers were being destroyed. Mother loved all animals, but she was adamant that we should be at least 11 years old and able to look after an animal.

So now the time had come and all of us, including the Great Aunt went on the tram to the Spring Street Dogs Home to choose a dog. We found a lovely male dog, about 18 months old. He was a terrier type mongrel, black, tan and white called Rover. We all agreed he was the dog we should adopt.

In those days there was very little traffic, which was a good job because he was Rover by name and Rover by nature, but he was always there waiting for his dinner.

On our first holiday we took him to stay in kennels at Ringinglow for a week. Transport was few and far between and it was a good three miles walk to the kennels to collect Rover after the holiday, and he was very pleased to see us. The following day, a Sunday, we let him out in the garden and he disappeared, we looked everywhere for him, going round all the usual walks, but no sign of him, on going home Mother had just received a telephone call from the kennels, to tell us Rover had arrived back at the kennels, we think he must have missed the company of the other dogs. Once again we had to walk three miles to Ringinglow, Rover was very pleased to see us, and became a reformed character!

Those of our age group will never forget the winter of 1947. We remember waking up to the windows and doors being covered during the night with mounds of snow. When we carefully opened the back door, the

Rover enjoying the garden

drifted snow fell in the house and we had to shovel and tunnel our way through the snow drifts. The snow was four feet deep in places and deeper where the wind had caused severe drifting. The city came to a standstill, all the schools were closed. The farmers worked with tractors and snow ploughs clearing the outskirts of Sheffield, whilst in the city centre, lorries with snow ploughs tried to clear the streets. With so much snow, it took a long time to do.

Bear in mind we had no central heating in those days, the toilet froze and we had to have a paraffin lamp in the bathroom all the time, which had to be trimmed and filled with paraffin daily. The bedrooms were particularly cold and when you opened the curtains you couldn't see out of the windows, which were covered with 'Jack Frost', admittedly it made lovely patterns on the windows.

Many houses had back-to-back fireplaces, and the oven in the kitchen was heated by the open coal fire in the dining room, which had to be backed up each night with slack - small pieces of coal mixed with coal dust

to try and keep the fire in overnight. It was important always to have a fire guard in front of the open fire in case it sent out sparks. The coal house was outside, so we quickly had to clear the snow to get coal and sticks for the fire.

We had a sledge, stored in the loft, which we had to get out, the roads were ideal for sledging, we put a box on the sledge to carry shopping home. When the main roads became clearer, the schools were able to re-open and the tram cars were able to run, also some of the bus routes were passable.

The side roads were still impassable and wellingtons were in short supply following the war, so Pat, borrowed a pair of heavy golf shoes from one of the neighbours and fastened brown paper round her legs for her journey to school.

In spite of the atrocious weather we seemed to get back to something resembling normality, quite quickly making the best of a bad job, if possible using trams or buses, but mainly walking or sledging.

Sunday school had continued all the time, and Muriel became one of the Sunday school teachers. One of the older teachers had never been on a sledge and was keen to have a go, so after Sunday school we all went to a nearby hilly road with no traffic and she thoroughly enjoyed her first experience of sledging.

Many people suffered hardship from burst pipes, leading to a shortage of water. Muriel remembers the dental practice on City Road, with the toilet at the bottom of the yard was frozen for weeks, and they had to use the next door's toilet. The snow falls continued periodically, and the hard ice was so thick that the lakes were safe for skating. It was well into March before the thaw started and the enormous lumps of ice were very slow to melt.

Following Pat's visit with the guides to London, we decided the following year to try and find a reasonably priced Bed and Breakfast, looking in a book we found a very cheap one in Sussex Gardens. Little did we know that the area didn't have a good reputation, but to be fair to them, we had no complaints, it was clean and we had a good breakfast. We visited a Lyon's Corner House for lunch and made sandwiches for later on. It was amazing how much we saw in the few days we were there, even though we were a bit foot sore. We had a great time visiting Buckingham Palace for the changing of the guards, the Tower of London, Westminster Abbey, St Paul's Cathedral with the Whispering Gallery, the Houses of Parliament with Big Ben, the famous wax works, the Cenotaph and 10 Downing Street, as well as taking a river trip on the Thames.

We returned home with many happy memories. Rover had to go in the kennels, which was the last time, as soon after that the owner retired, so it was closed down.

New beginnings

Muriel's Dental career with Mr Fyffe was very different and enjoyable after her experience at Alderson Road. On the first day I walked down to Mr Fyffe's home at Millhouses with my packed lunch time sandwiches and my new white coat to be taken by car to the practice at 38 City Road. After this first day I was given a key to the practice to make my own way there.

City Road was part of long straight ribbon road which began at Duke Street opposite the fruit and vegetable market, in about a mile it changed to City Road which continued as far as Manor Top, climbing all the way. Tram cars went all the way up to Manor Top, then turned down Prince of Wales Road. Most of the properties were terrace houses, two rooms downstairs and an off-shoot kitchen, two rooms upstairs and an attic, the toilet was at the bottom of the garden.

There was a small porch at number 38, with an outside door and a second door with a bell, which I answered many times a day. The front room on the right of the hallway was the surgery, also on the right of the hall was a steep staircase to the upstairs rooms. At the end of the hall there was a step down into the waiting room, where there was a desk and the telephone, a further door led to a step down into the kitchen and the back door on the left, there were two steps into the small garden, which Mr Jackson, our neighbour, looked after. Mr and Mrs Jackson ran a window cleaning business so our windows were kept shining clean.

The upstairs front room was a store room for books and junk. The back upstairs room was the dental laboratory where artificial dentures were made. The plaster bench was in the corner and I soon learnt how to cast models in Plaster of Paris.

Like all dental laboratories, the bench had a hole about seven inches square with a bucket underneath to catch waste plaster when you cleaned the mixing bowl. This bucket was emptied most lunchtimes in the outside bin. There was also a metal press to squeeze the flasks together when constructing dentures. The next bench had a gas ring for boiling the kettle and a vulcanizer, which incorporated a gas ring and was used to cook Vulcanite dentures or do repair work, similar to a pressure cooker. At the end of the bench was an electric polishing lathe for finishing dentures and repairs. The materials used were pumice and whitening, which were mixed with water to allay dust. The lathe had a twelve inch grooved spindle to which you attached various brushes and buffs. It was a messy job due to the speed of the lathe and I had to wear a mask, spectacles and cover my chest and head with old towels to protect myself from dust. The long bench by the window had two bunsen burners and various small tools including wax knives, and an electric motor for trimming the final denture.

Downstairs the surgery was a 1930s replica, there was a stand on which stood a water sterilizer. My first job every morning was to fill this and put the instruments in to boil, my last job at night was to take the instruments out and empty the water. There were no antibiotics, we used salt and water mouthwashes which worked well. It sounds very crude by modern methods, but we rarely had any infection.

There was a nitrous oxide machine, which could be used for simple extractions in the early days, but then Mr Fyffe started bringing a more modern machine from home. I was quite competent at completing claim forms for insurance claims and can still remember the huge pile awaiting attention. This, of course, was eighteen months before the start of the National Health Service on 5th July 1948, when every man, woman and child became entitled to free dental treatment.

Muriel, Mother and Pat

In 1948 Pat took her GCE exams. I wasn't a total failure, but the results were very mediocre, so I returned to retake them in the autumn at the University, being in a strange environment didn't help and I wasn't happy with my efforts. I felt the time had come to leave school and get a job. If my results had been better I had thought about becoming a radiographer, but that wouldn't be possible now, so nothing ventured, nothing gained, I contacted the x-ray department at the Royal Hospital, and there was a vacancy for a junior dark room assistant.

I was asked to attend for interview with Dr. Grout, who was in charge of the department, elderly and rather stern. He asked me lots of questions about school and my family and I must have given the correct answers, because I was offered the job to start immediately, with an initial salary of £1-1shilling a week. I had to go to school to tell Dr Green, the Headmistress, that I was leaving and the details of the job I had been offered.

The work of a dark room assistant was to receive the x-rays in the dark room, take the x-ray out of the cassette and write the name of the patient with a pencil at the bottom of the x-ray, to begin with I found writing in the dark difficult. Then you fastened the x-ray in a frame and put it in the developer for a given time, then it had to be rinsed and put in a fixer, before being washed and dried. Then the four sharp corners had to be cut with a machine and finally the film was placed in a large brown envelope. The procedure is very different today.

The radiographer would come to be shown the x-ray to ensure it was satisfactory. As well as developing the x-rays taken in the department I also had to develop the x-rays taken in the casualty department, and the doctors would come to view the x-rays. I got quite good at reading the x-rays.

Working in the hospital and coming in contact with other people increased my interest in undertaking a nursing career. I spoke to my immediate senior, and she suggested that I should speak to Dr Grout. So in June 1949 I saw Dr Grout and said I would like to undertake nurse training. He walked me up and down the corridor talking to me and told me he would go and see the Matron and ask her to have a word with me. It all happened quickly and I was accepted to commence training in September 1949.

Muriel and Pat were due a weeks holiday and managed to get the same week off, Mother decided that we should have a seaside holiday and she found a very nice guest house in a magazine which would allow a dog to be taken, so a week-long holiday was booked at Woolacombe. Mother said we would send the luggage in advance in the large trunk, which normally lived under a bed upstairs. It was polished and packed a few days before, with all we would need for a week, it was locked and collected by the railway and was waiting for us in the bedroom when we arrived on the Saturday afternoon. Rover went with us so we only had his food dish and biscuits, plus sandwiches for the journey to carry.

On holiday at Woolacombe

The guest house was just across the road from the sea and miles of sand, we had a super holiday, we went on a boat trip and Rover had a great time paddling. It was lovely to visit an area of the country which was new to us and we returned home with many happy memories. The trunk was collected by the railway, which arrived back at Gisborne Road on the Monday. We came home on the train on the Saturday, ready for work on Monday.

Muriel soon realized her work at City Road involved the whole process of a dental surgery and the technical side too, learning to cast impressions that had been taken in the surgery. These had to be dealt with as quickly as possible, because the material used would shrink if left uncovered. A damp cloth had to cover the trays whilst in the surgery, and they were taken to the laboratory as soon as possible. A stone coloured plaster was mixed with water and poured onto the tray over the impression, this took about ten minutes to set. It was best not to leave them until they were partially set, then you could cut the excess plaster away with a knife. This was not always possible if the telephone or door bell rang, by the time you got back up stairs they would be hard.

The impressions were then usually left overnight and the next morning you had to gently prise them off to reveal a copy of the mouth in plaster. A hack-saw was used to trim round the edges so you could handle the model. Sheets of pink wax were softened over the Bunsen burner and placed over the plaster model, the spare wax was trimmed with a knife. The waste wax was collected in boxes and sent away to be cleaned and rolled into flat sheets for re-use. This was the first method of constructing a full or partial denture. It was only in the late 1940s that acrylic dentures were first started to be made.

Alternative material to rubber (vulcanite) had to be found when war commenced, when Japan entered the war there was an immediate cut off of supplies.

I remember some very cold winters, there was no central heating, just a two bar Belling electric radiator in the waiting room and the surgery, plus an electric water heater over the surgery sink for hand washing. In the laboratory there was just a cold water tap, with a kettle and saucepan on the gas ring the only means of hot water. I soon found out that long sleeved white overalls in the winter were essential so that you could have something warm underneath. I used to have chilblains on both hands and feet, so I wore warm socks over my tights and kept my outdoor shoes on all day. The chilblains on my hands itched terribly and were red and swollen, sometimes becoming broken. I painted a plastic skin on them, which did help.

Our local chemist made a prescription of Opodeldoc and Glycerine to rub on at night, which was wonderful for dry skin, caused through working with Plaster and frequent hand washing in the surgery with insufficient drying. Unfortunately, this cannot be made up now due to the basic ingredient being withdrawn by the European Union in the 21st Century. Despite these problems, I loved my work.

I found out that there was a Dental Nurse Society with their headquarters in Leyland, Lancashire, so I wrote to find out more and discovered there was a section in Sheffield and I could learn and study to get my Certificate A exam.

During late 1947 Pat and Muriel both became involved in the St John Ambulance Brigade. We realised there was an interest in first aid, we had both taken first aid and home nursing exams - Muriel as an adult and Pat as a cadet - so we wrote to the local schools inviting those interested to come to a meeting in the Ecclesall Memorial Rooms on a Wednesday night at 6:15pm. Several children attended prior to the adult meeting at 8pm. This was useful as we managed to share their equipment which saved money.

It was in March 1948 that fourteen girls were enrolled in the first enrolment ceremony, and made their promises 'to serve God and all mankind'. Little did we realise that this was going to take every minute of spare time.

Meanwhile Pat had continued as a girl guide until the early part of 1949 and the experience she had gained held her in good stead with the cadet division. In the six years as a guide, she had taken every opportunity to go camping with her patrol group, as well as the larger camps. The last guide camp she attended was in 1948, at Treaddur Bay, Anglesey, by chance they were short of a Camp Nurse. Muriel, who filled the bill with her adult first aid and home nursing certificates, came as camp nurse, although a first time camper she also gained a lot of experience.

Off to camp with the Guides. Muriel came as Camp Nurse

1949

When you became a student nurse in 1949, you had to live in, therefore married ladies were not encouraged. Pat's training began with three months in the School of Nursing alongside students training at the Royal Hospital, the Royal Infirmary or the Children's Hospital, we took this initial training together, so there were around sixty in the class at the Clarkehouse Road School.

Some of us, including myself, were accommodated in Ranfall, one of the large houses on Ranmoor Park Road; four or us shared a large bedroom. The Principal of the School of Nursing and some of the tutors also lived in Ranfall, it was about a two mile walk to the School of Nursing. We all wore the same uniform, which was provided, for our three months in Preliminary Training School, a short sleeved blue dress with a white collar and white edging on the sleeves, and a white nurses cap, which on our first day we were instructed how they should be folded and worn. Our foot wear was black stockings and black lace up shoes.

The course covered all aspects of nursing care: hygiene, dietetics, first aid, anatomy and physiology and practical experience. Once a week we had to wear shorts and a t-shirt for keep fit exercises, I think he was a physiotherapist who took this class. Most of the lectures were at Clarkehouse with a variety of lecturers, on the occasional Saturday morning we went to Sheffield University for anatomy and physiology lectures, which included dissecting cadavers- quite gruesome!

At the end of the three months training we had to sit six-hour long exam papers, plus a practical examination. If you did not pass, that was the end of your aim to become a State Registered Nurse. Fortunately, I think most of us were successful and we were allowed a short break before commencing at the hospital of our choice.

The first Dental Nurses' Association A.G.M. Muriel attended

When I became a member of the Dental Nurses' Association in 1947, I quickly realised that the dental nurse was the Cinderella of the dental profession. However, in Sheffield, we had an active membership with an enthusiastic secretary, Miss

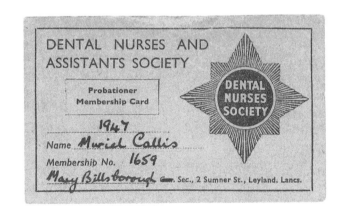

Mary McKenzie. Members came from Sheffield, Rotherham, Doncaster and

Nottinghamshire, and we all met in a room at The Grand Hotel on Leopold Street, Sheffield, once a month on a Sunday afternoon. Members came from different types of the profession: private practice, hospitals, local authority clinics. The meetings usually commenced with a short business meeting followed by a speaker, who was often a Dental Surgeon, or a demonstration of a new product.

We formed a study group, meeting in different dental practices to gain more knowledge. Previous exam papers were obtained for practise; we marked each other's papers and were very critical with comments. This was very interesting and helpful in our work, especially the naming of instruments and their uses, which varied in different practices. It took me two years of studying in my spare time before I felt ready to sit the exam. Several of us from Sheffield went to Leeds Dental Hospital for the exam which was in two parts: in the morning we had a three hour written paper, followed by a practical test in the afternoon. I passed the examination, although several were not successful and had to wait a further twelve months before they could re-sit the exam.

The highlight of the society was the Annual General Meeting, which was held in different areas during the Easter Holiday weekend. Those who had gained a certificate during the year were presented after the Annual Dinner on the Saturday by a local dignitary such as the Lord Mayor. These weekends were packed with lectures and possibly a visit to a dental hospital, sometimes we were able to observe surgery. There were trade stands with the latest equipment and materials for us to visit and the goodie bag was always packed with interesting items to take home.

On Easter Sunday, quite a number of us would go to the 8am Holy Communion Service at a nearby church. A number of members wore special Easter hats on the Sunday when they attended the Annual General Meeting, which was chaired by the outgoing President who, following the business part of the meeting, then installed the new President. Before lunch everyone would gather for the official photograph to be taken. Members who were able to stay until Monday enjoyed sight seeing arranged by the host members, before wending their way home.

With the advent of the National Health Service on 5th July 1948 everyone in the United Kingdom was eligible for free dental treatment. It received a fair amount of publicity, so people arrived in vast numbers. We soon realised that extra help was required in the laboratory due to the increase of patients requiring new dentures. I had a waiting list for dentures, which we limited the number taken each week. As I had to devote more time in the surgery and the office, Mr Fyffe approached George, a dental technician who had served an apprenticeship previously. He wished to come back and he remained in the practice for about seven years.

In St John officer uniform with Mother

Training days

At the end of the preliminary training we were transferred to the main nurses' home - Tapton Court on Fulwood Road. There we had single rooms and received bus tokens for our journey to the Royal Hospital, West Street. Our uniform was a white short sleeved dress and belt, the colour of which depicted whether we were a first, second or third year student. We then wore a green coat, green beret, black stockings and black laced up shoes, plus a green cloak with a red lining. We had a pittance of a salary which took into account the fact that we were provided with accommodation and food.

There were three shifts: the early shift ran from 7:30am to 4pm, the late shift from 12:30pm to 9pm, or a split shift which ran 7.30am to noon then 4pm to 9pm - we had one half day and one day off per week. On the early shift we had a 15-minute break between 9am and 9:30am, when we would dash to the dining room for a drink and a slice of toast and dripping, then we had a half an hour break for a main meal. It was a wonder if we ever got off the ward on time and we soon learnt to swallow our meal as quickly as possible.

The first ward I worked on was a male medical ward and the previous junior on the ward was very quick to show me how to collect, empty and boil the sputum mugs! The ward sister was very strict, when it was time to go off duty we went to the office to ask permission to go and she would come out onto the ward to ensure we had done all our tasks. In particular, if we were on a late shift at 9pm we had to make sure there were no newspapers visible, the counter panes were straight with the hospital

Nurses on the step at The School of Nursing on Clarkehouse Road.
Pat is on the bottom step at the far right

emblem in the centre and the central bed wheels were facing the correct way. We worked extremely hard and were exhausted by bed time.

The wards all had their own cleaners and a ward orderly who did the daily cleaning, but once a week, after the doctors had done their rounds, it was all hands on deck. The beds on one side of the ward were all pushed to the centre and the area cleaned, including the beds, before they were pushed back, then the other side received the same treatment and finally the entire central area was cleaned. If it was a wooden floor, such as the eye ward, the floors were polished until they shone. There was an electric polisher, but one of the sisters didn't think they did the job as well as the polishers you had to do manually and she showed us how it should be done!

After working days for six to eight months, the change list would go up to say we would be going on night duty for up to three months. At 8:30pm we had to be outside the night sister's office to be told the ward we had to

All the Student nurses from the Royal Hospital and the Royal Infirmary
with their tutors on a study week

work on. As a junior pro we had to run between two wards, there being a
second or third year nurse in charge of the ward. If the ward was
particularly busy there may have been two nurses allocated. The wards
were all Nightingale wards with at least between 20 to 32 patients to care
for and you were expected to know the name and diagnosis of every
patient. One of the night sisters would come round the ward twice during
the night, the first time was about 10pm and woe betide you if the main
lights were not out.

During our early training we were given Mantoux tests to exclude
tuberculosis. Soon after this I developed corneal ulcers and was referred to
Mr Mackie, the Consultant in the eye department, who immediately
admitted me to a side ward on the Bingham Ward for Ophthalmic patients;
for treatment of the corneal ulcers. I was in hospital about ten days,
followed by ten days at home.

It was decided that I was allergic to Mantoux tests and I had to have an injection monthly for about three or four months to desensitise me. The ulcers were painful, particularly in a bright light, so I wore an eye shade for some weeks, you can imagine the comments I had! On return from sick leave I worked on the eye ward so that I could continue receiving treatment. Although this put me back in my training, it didn't really matter because you could not take your finals until you had reached your 21st birthday. I had started my training when I was seventeen and a half, so I had to wait until June 1953 to take my finals.

I enjoyed working on the eye ward, methods were very different to the modern treatment, for example following a cataract operation the patient was kept in bed with double eye bandages, and to treat glaucoma we applied a leech. When the leech was not in use, it was kept in a container of water on the ward desk, and it would make you jump when it made a quick movement.

Every ward was very different: the Ear, Nose and Throat ward had its own Theatre and operation day was hectic, with up to ten children being admitted at 8am for the removal of their tonsils. The children were about five to ten years of age, and there were lots of tears when the mothers had to leave them. I can remember one little boy had hob nailed boots on and he kicked like mad. When they came back from theatre, they had to be given one of the Sulphonamides crushed in water, it was so difficult to get them to drink it and they frequently brought it all back.

The male Accident and Emergency ward was on the ground floor, we frequently had men who had had an accident in the mines and they would be covered with lime dust. The men, when they were recovering, were a cheerful lot, they could also get us in trouble by sneaking cigarettes, particularly during the night, which was a hazard.

One of the hardest wards was the female medical ward, which had over thirty patients, there were two side wards, a large open plan ward and an extra ward at the far end with about eight or ten beds. I worked on the ward during my third night duty and one night there were three deaths, not easy in a Nightingale type ward - you had to close the curtains and put screens to make a pathway to go to the mortuary.

We all had to spend some time in the operating theatre, which I enjoyed, but it was very different in the 1940s and 50s. We were responsible for cleaning and sterilising the equipment, and the Surgeons each had their own likes and dislikes. Whilst on my third night duty, one of the night sisters came to ask me to go theatre and prepare and scrub for an emergency operation. The Surgeon was Irish man, who always had his own instruments in a bag, so these had to be sterilised. He also had a reputation for throwing things if anything was wrong, fortunately everything went well, much to my relief!

During our training we had two study weeks in the second and third year at the Clarkehouse School of Nursing. We all had a long form, on which was written every possible procedure, at the side there was a space for Sister or Staff Nurse to sign when we had been taught that particular procedure, and another space stating that we were proficient performing the procedure.

We also had to spend a period of time working on the Gynaecological ward at the Jessop Hospital for Women and at the Children's Hospital. The Royal Hospital also had an annexe at Fulwood, which had a variety of patients, some were patients requiring long term care, some were having skin grafts and there was a male ward and a female ward for neuro-medical cases.

Our work with the Ecclesall St John Cadet Division had continued to thrive and we were anxious to take the cadets camping after I had completed my general training in 1953. But in 1952 Pat needed to go on a St John Camp Training course which ran from Friday tea time until Sunday lunch time, and student nurses were not allowed to have weekend days off, these were reserved for trained staff.

The only chance would be to ask Matron if I could have a Saturday day off. It was not the done thing, but she relented on the condition that I would have to be on duty on the Sunday. Fortunately, because I had been camping several times with the girl guides, I was allowed to attend the course from the Friday night to Saturday teatime.

So off I went with my kit bag to a field in Blackburn, Lancashire. It was pitch black when I arrived and was shown to the tent where I was to sleep with three other members, all a little older than me. We were up bright and early the next morning to get breakfast, and it was soon obvious that I had more experience than most on the course. It was a mixed course, male and female, and those having breakfast had to smother their laughter when one the men came to request some hot water to shave! We had talks on the setting up of a camp, and after lunch there was a practical session on camp activities, including games to play with the cadets. All too quickly it was time for me to leave, the Officer taking the course, admitted that I knew, as much, if not more than he knew about camping, and I received a certificate saying that I had attended the course.

Towards the end of my last night duty, the Night Sister told me that the Matron wanted to see me in the morning. You always wonder what you had done wrong! On this occasion it was to tell me that I had been awarded the Chairman's Prize for making steady, good progress during my training, needless to say I was delighted but shattered to be receiving a special award.

The Annual Prize Giving Ceremony at the City Hall. Pat was awarded the Chairman's Prize, which was a Midwifery Book. Pat is third from the left on the bottom row

The annual prize giving for the United Sheffield Hospitals School of Nursing took place at the City Hall on 9th December 1952 at 2:30pm. Those who had completed their three years of training at the Royal Hospital and the Royal Infirmary during that year received our Certificates of Training and I received my prize - a midwifery book. I would be undertaking my midwifery training after I had taken my State Registration exams to become a State Registered Nurse, when I was 21-years-old.

The exams took place in June 1953, two days after the Queen's Coronation. At this time I was working at Fulwood Annexe and a television had been acquired for the patients to watch the events in London, unfortunately they could not get the TV to work. I had a half day and remember walking home to watch the highlights of the day on the 10inch TV screen Muriel and I had brought on hire purchase - the only time we ever used hire purchase. Several friends came to watch the coronation with us and Mother had made a buffet style meal, it was a very happy occasion.

I received my badge from the General Nursing Council for England and Wales with my number 204044, dated 27.7.53 and engraved P.M. Callis S.R.N. (State Registered Nurse). It was a very proud day. A few weeks later I received a certificate and uniform permit.

When I first started my training, Mother had bought me a nurse's fob watch, with a second hand for taking pulse rates. It was in constant use throughout my 40 years working life in the Health Service. Sadly, when it needed repairing, none of the watch repairers could get the spare parts, so I was unable to wear it. Recently a good friend, who lives locally, repaired it and I now proudly wear it every day.

L. drivers

In the early 1950s Muriel thought a car would be useful and we should have driving lessons. She applied for a provisional licence and booked a course of lessons but soon realised that without a car it was not going to be easy and she was putting the cart before the horse!

Where would we park a car? Could we afford a car and how much would it cost? The parking of the car was the most important, and at that time we had a single gate and pathway up to our house, but there would be room for a double driveway. Part of the boundary wall would have to be taken down, the laurel bushes and privet hedge would have to be taken out. We had a trellis gateway with a rose tree on the garden side, plus a trellis between our house and our neighbours house. The area where the Anderson Shelter and blast wall had been during the war would be adequate for the garage. It would be quite a long drive - three times the length of the house.

Undaunted, we two girls started to do the work. Needless to say we received plenty of advice from our neighbours and passers by. Removing the various bushes, trees and trellises was hard work, but we got the area cleared, including moving piles of soil to other parts of the garden. The wall was different, we tried a crow bar and even sawing through it! Eventually we had to capitulate and as the relatives of our neighbours were builders, they removed the stones and flattened the area where the garage would be situated.

We became very proficient in mixing cement, most of it by hand, although we did borrow a cement mixer when we laid the garage floor.

Of course, all this work had to be fitted in with Muriel working full time at the dentist and Pat completing her general training and midwifery training.

At the same time that all this was happening, we had a thriving St John Cadet Division, our numbers increased as children from different areas of Sheffield heard about Ecclesall Cadets and came from the Manor, Heeley, Lodge Moor and Fulwood. We encouraged the cadets to attend church parades once a month with the other organisations. The cadets had a wide range of activities which included all aspects of first aid, home nursing including bandaging and bed making; we also took them on rambles, cooked outdoors and played lots of games.

The first Camp, we were short of adults so Mother came as Camp Nurse

In 1951 HRH Princess Margaret, our Commandant-in-Chief, came to Doncaster for a large rally on Doncaster Race Course, attended by all the cadet divisions from a wide area, including Ecclesall Cadet Division. Muriel was in charge and it was a memorable day. On several other occasions we were asked to provide Guards of Honour, one was the opening of the new Rowlinson School in 1953.

The cadets' exams in first aid and home nursing were taken by a Doctor and a trained Nurse. Competitive work in first aid and home nursing was exciting for all of us, and a good way of putting what the cadets had been taught into a realistic situation.

Pat was keen to take the cadets camping, as she had gained her camping warrant in 1952, so in August 1953 we held our first camp at Filey. We hired a Sheffield United tour bus to take us and our equipment. The tentage was delivered from Langdon's and was waiting for us when we arrived. For this first camp we took 21 cadets who were all new to camping and in the weeks prior to the camp, it was like training for a survival course. The older cadets were in charge of a group of five or six in one bell tent and we had given prior preparation on pitching tents, cooking over an open fire, the best wood to make a good fire and a whole host of requirements. All camps had to be inspected by a senior member of the Brigade in the Area where we were camping, and we had an excellent report. As this was a new experience, we had a number of visitors, who were all impressed with what they saw. This was to be the first of many camps!

To be a midwife!

In September 1953 Pat commenced her Midwifery Training which was in two parts. Part one, which took six months, was at the Jessop Hospital, and I had to be resident in the nurses' home, a short walk from the hospital. Part one started with a short intensive period in the Midwifery Training School, followed by regular study days with lectures from the Obstetricians, Paediatricians and the Midwifery Tutors; and gaining experience on all the wards including the labour suite.

We had to witness ten normal deliveries before we were allowed to deliver a baby under the watchful eye of one of the Sisters or Staff Midwives. In order to witness deliveries, as soon as we heard a mother was in the second stage of labour we rushed to labour suite, hoping to be there in time. We were very grateful to the mothers for allowing us to watch at this important time. As part of our training we had to write up five case histories of mothers we had delivered.

The pain relief drugs we mainly used were Seconal, which was given in the very early stages, plus Potassium bBromide and Chloral Hydrate, Pethidine or occasionally Heroin; gas and air was widely used. Mothers past their expected date, were given a medical induction of 2ozs of castor oil, an enema, and a bath!

In the 1950s, mothers stayed on the post-natal ward much longer than nowadays - the baby's cord had separated and feeding was established before discharge, which could be eight to ten days or more after the birth. The Matron at the Jessop Hospital was Miss Taylor, who was very strict and it was known that she may ask the switch board telephonist for an early call, to

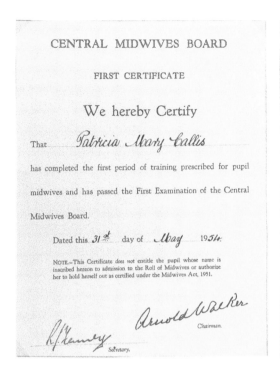

CENTRAL MIDWIVES BOARD

FIRST CERTIFICATE

We hereby Certify

That _Patricia Mary Callis_

has completed the first period of training prescribed for pupil

midwives and has passed the First Examination of the Central

Midwives Board.

Dated this 31st day of _May_ 1954.

NOTE.—This Certificate does not entitle the pupil whose name is
inscribed hereon to admission to the Roll of Midwives or authorize
her to hold herself out as certified under the Midwives Act, 1951.

Arnold Walker
Chairman.

R. Kenney
Secretary.

CENTRAL MIDWIVES BOARD

No. _139096_   Date _20th December_ 1954.

We hereby Certify

That _Patricia Mary Callis_

having passed the First and Second Examinations of the
Central Midwives Board, and having otherwise complied
with the rules made in pursuance of the Midwives Act,
1951, is entitled by law to practise as a Midwife in
accordance with the provisions of the said Act and subject
to the said rules.

Arnold Walker
Chairman.

R. Kenney
Secretary.

surprise the night staff. Fortunately, the telephonist would drop a hint to the night staff.

Christmas was always an exciting time and it was rare not to have a baby born that day - the press would come to take pictures of the babies being proudly held by the pupil midwives.

Our six months was nearly at an end when I developed a high temperature and was sent home, because the Assistant Matron rightly thought my mother would look after me better. The next day, the Doctor for all staff visited to ensure I was alright. With the help of Mother's old remedies I soon recovered and was back at work. All too soon the exams came round, these were set by the Central Midwives' Board and there were written papers and a practical exam.

It was with great relief that I received my first certificate, stating that I had passed the first examination of the Central Midwives' Board, on the 31st May 1954. Some pupils only took the first examination, which allowed them to take the Health Visitor Training course. To quote: "The certificate does not entitle the pupil, whose name is inscribed hereon to admission to the Roll of

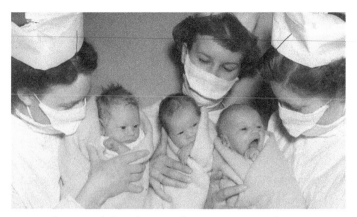

Christmas babies born at the Jessop Hospital 1953.
Pat is holding the hungry one!

Midwives or authorize her to hold herself out as Certified under the Midwives Act, 1951."

In other words, to become a midwife, I had to take Part Two of the training, so in June 1954, I commenced Part Two at Nether Edge Maternity Unit.

This was a much smaller unit than the Jessop Hospital, the mothers were mainly booked through the local authority clinic. We had a weekly study day and during the first three months we had to write six comprehensive case histories. I was able to be non-resident for the first three months.

The case books, containing forms and charts were prepared and issued by the Central Midwives' Board. Copyright is reserved, so we had to treat them with great respect and not make any mistakes.

After the first three months we were allocated to live with a community midwife. About six or eight of us were sent to a midwife in the West Ring of Yorkshire, I went to Pontefract, so we had a train journey to reach our destination. I was very fortunate with the Midwife and family that I lived with, a Mr and Mrs Pritchard and their ten-year-old daughter, Margaret. It was a very happy household and Mrs Pritchard was a good cook. Fortunately, this was long before I became a vegetarian, and I can remember several Yorkshire dishes that I had never tasted before, such as black pudding and soused herring, but I tried them all. We had been brought up to always eat up and I really did enjoy everything I had, much to Mrs Pritchard's relief.

Once again we had to write up six district case histories, which was very laborious and I still had to go into Sheffield for the weekly study day. The district wasn't as busy as I would have liked it to be, particularly as I was hoping to become a district midwife, but it was a very enjoyable three months.

In December we sat our final exams, and on the 20th December 1954, I received my Certificate and number 139096 from the Central Midwives' Board. I was now entitled to practise as a Midwife in accordance with the Midwives Act of 1951 and subject to the said rules.

I had applied to the Sheffield Health Authority for the post of District Midwife and, following an interview with one of the Health Authority Doctors and the Supervisor of Midwives, I was accepted to start on 1st January 1955.

My uniform was ordered and I received all the required equipment, this included: an antenatal bag, a delivery bag, the drugs I was allowed to carry, a dozen white gowns, a register of cases, a large diary, a supply of delivery boxes, various forms and other information, also the weighty gas and air machine. It became a priority that I should have driving lessons and aim to pass my driving test as soon as possible.

We had purchased our first car in 1954, an Austin Big Seven OD 9941, which cost £50, and

Pat the Midwife in indoor and outdoor uniforms

various friends offered tuition. There was a large area of land at Lodge Moor, where the prisoner of war camp had been during the war. We could practise reversing and three point turns, we also had lessons from a driving school. It was a bit of a blow when I had to go to Pontefract, so I decided I would have a go at the driving test, for experience, although I knew I wasn't ready. We only kept OD 9941 for a short time and sold it for £50. At the end of 1954, we changed driving schools and by the beginning of March 1955 we both passed our driving tests. We then purchased a second hand Ford Anglia EKY 30, it was a great relief for Pat, not having to use public transport.

Spreading our wings

During the early 1950s we had contact with relatives in America. Mother had spent about five years working in America and Canada, before and at the beginning of World War One. There were cousins who had emigrated to America and Mother used to visit them during this time. In the 1950s cousin Jessie with her American husband Joe spent a holiday in England, staying with us for part of the visit. It was great fun hearing about the USA, and taking them round the old places. They were great Canasta players and they taught us the card game.

Our St John cadet division continued to thrive and after the success of the camp at Filey, we wanted to make camping an annual event; we had been unable to have a camp in 1954, due to Pat's midwifery training commitments.

Living together for a week, under canvas, was a great character building experience for the cadets, we got to know them and the cadets got to know the leaders, so in 1955 we booked a camp site at Conway.

There is a great amount of preparation when you are taking 30 to 40 children and adults for a weeks camping holiday, you have to prepare well in advance, to avoid disappointment. The tentage had to be booked from Langdon's of Liverpool, we needed six or seven bell tents, a 24ft by 12ft marquee, a large ridge tent for the cooks, a ridge tent for the first aid tent and wash tents. We made the latrine screening ourselves, using hessian, as well as the waterproof screening for the cooking fire. We had acquired several large tea chests, which could double up as a table; two large galvanised dustbins, which were used to heat the water for washing; several washing up bowls; four large dixies and two billies; a saw and large axe, plus many other utensils.

We all had our kitbag, containing the normal requirements and sleeping bags, plus we each had our own unbreakable dish, plates and cutlery. We had to have menus planned for the week and either take some items with us or arrange ordering. Transport had to be booked and luggage labels made out for any luggage going in advance.

In order to run a camp, we were to have the required one adult to ten children, so there was Skipper, the Quarter Master (quem), an assistant quem and a camp nurse, as a minimum. There were six cadets in a bell tent, under the supervision of a leader and a second. Each day they were responsible, in turn, for certain tasks: cooks, wood, water, orderly and health sections – who looked after the latrines! There was a daily tent inspection, to make sure everything was off the ground, supported on wood gadgets, and the brailing was rolled up to air the tent, as long as it wasn't raining.

The order of the day was a reveille whistle at 7am, followed by raising the flag, and prayers at 7:30am, breakfast at 8am, dinner at 12:30pm, and tea at 5pm. There would be some variation depending on our programme, and we aimed to get everyone to bed by 9pm.

We hired a Sheffield United Tours coach to take us to Conway, but when the driver saw the narrow bridge he had to pass through, he nearly turned back. His wing mirrors had to be turned in, and Pat had to guide him through and we all held our breath. It was a lovely site, owned by a friendly Welsh farmer. We had superb weather and were able visit the smallest house on the jetty, the lighthouse and we had a bus to take us to Holyhead. The camp inspection went well and a good time was had by all.

In 1956 we decided to go to Dolgellau, mid Wales, by train. The field was on a slight slope, well above sea level, and we got everything pitched in fine weather, although every night we had strong winds which came up the Afton Mawddach Estuary and landed on our camp site!

The weather was reasonable the first half of the week. At the camp inspection the inspector wanted to pitch one of the tents using a different method of pitching, he showed us what to do, although we were not very impressed.

That night the wind was gale force and it started to rain, a little voice came

Waiting to get on the train for Dolgellau

to our tent: "Skip…our tent has blown down." There was only one guess which tent it was - the one the inspector pitched!

The cadets were quickly settled in the other tents and we ensured the blown down tent was secure, then attempted to go to sleep. When morning came the tent was re-pitched and although the weather was deteriorating life in camp continued, this was our last day prior to striking camp, and everyone made the best of it, even singing the camp fire songs in the marquee, and it was early to bed.

About 3am, a little voice at our tent said: "our tent is flooded." The innocent looking brook at the top of the field decided to change its course right under one of the tents, there was a quick reorganisation of the tents for the remaining part of the night and all except the officers went to sleep.

There was a gale blowing and our tent, which we had borrowed, had a centre pole that was too long. Although we had made a hole for it to sit in, we spent the rest of the night knocking in the brailing pegs. A lovely dawn brought daylight, and we were up early to discover the fire place completely flooded.

All our uniforms for going home in were put in plastic bags to keep them dry, and the cadets packed their kitbags. Skipper and some of the older cadets started to take down the wet tents, putting them at the entrance to the field, ready for the lorry to pick them up. Meanwhile, Muriel and her helpers fed everyone, a few at a time, with cereals and scrambled eggs, cooked on an enamel plate on a small methylated spirit stove, plus bread and butter and a drink.

What a superb lot of cadets, they worked like Trojans, and we all arrived at the station in time for the train. When the train started we went two at a time into the toilet to wash and put on our uniforms, the result was stunning and nobody would have known that we had camped in such atrocious weather. The station master congratulated us on being the only campers in the area who had stayed the full week. The cadets had a great time, with so much excitement!

On arriving home, we had a busy time ahead, preparing teams to enter for competitions, this was very exciting, particularly when we became more experienced and came home with the cup.

We were invited to the opening of the new Police Headquarters by Lady Louis Mountbatten, as our Commandant In Chief, she combined the visit with meeting the St John Cadets, who put on displays of the work of the cadets, particularly first aid, home nursing and camping, which was well received.

Finally, at this time the parents formed a very active Parents' Association, which provided us with financial support.

Showing our demonstrations to
Lady Louis Mountbatten

The End of Part 1.

Part II

1956

The Superintendent of the Sunday School, Miss Slater, asked Muriel if she would consider becoming a Sunday School teacher. I was delighted to be asked, little did I realise that I would continue teaching for about 30 years!

Pat also became a teacher but because of her chosen career, only for about four years. One of the teachers had spent some time in the mission field and it was fun listening to her experiences. She helped organise one of the concerts, where the children dressed to represent different countries. Unfortunately, due to family commitments, she had to leave the area.

The picture shows where we met in the church hall, Miss Slater is on the right and as you can see she was not in the best of health.

Gradually over the years I took over more responsibility. When I became Superintendent I was asked to represent the Kindergarten Sunday school on the Parochial Church Council, this enabled me to ask for a grant each year to provide lesson books and equipment for the Kindergarten.

The Kindergarten age group was three to eight years of age, they then transferred to the junior class. The curates always took an active interest, one of the early ones was Rev Peter Wright. The teachers used to go to his house for study groups; he, his wife and family were a delight, but of course the curates soon moved on.

Another curate was Rev Jack Milverton, he held preparation classes once a month, with extra notes for each week. Safeguarding children was always a priority at Ecclesall, but it did not involve going to expensive courses and DBS checks. It was down to earth common sense - you knew your staff, and you would never be on your own with a child in a room with the door shut!

The Sunday school was never short of teachers but sometimes lacked a pianist. Muriel, who had never had a music lesson, but had a good ear for music, used to fill in. There were around 100 children on the register and we knew all the parents. The children brought their pennies each week and the money was sent to the Missionary Society.

Rev Milverton was also an excellent pastoral visitor, he visited our mother when she was ill and you could hear their laughter well before you got to our house.

Following the initial rush brought on by the NHS, in the late fifties and early sixties the Dental Practice work had settled down to an easier pace. Some charges had been levied on certain treatments by the government. This included dentures, which slowed down this type of work. The technician, George, decided that there was insufficient work for him to stay full time, so he went back to his previous job as a motor mechanic. We missed him, he was such a cheerful character, but we all still kept in touch.

I was never required to work at night with Mr Fyffe, so I finished at 5pm, this enabled me to go to night school to attend a Dental Mechanics Course and I went for two years. I enjoyed the practical side and learnt many things from the others on the course. I found I wasn't the only female who did mechanical work and enjoyed swapping ideas.

As a member of the Dental Nurses' Association, I took a great interest in the meetings and at the AGM of the local branch, the previous treasurer was not seeking re-election. As usual, the treasurer is always a difficult role to fill, I eventually allowed my name to go forward and was duly elected treasurer of the Sheffield section.

I have always been eternally grateful to Mother for sending me to Whiteleys Business College, where I learnt bookkeeping and business methods, skills which have served me well.

My first big job was the national AGM, which was being held in Sheffield as one of our members, Mary Mackenzie, had been elected the previous Easter as President. The Sheffield section made all the preparations to host the 1956 AGM. We all worked well as a committee for this event and I was able to show that we had managed to cover all our expenses.

We held the annual dinner at the Albany Hotel, Surrey Street. Our chief guest was the Lord Mayor of Sheffield, Ald. J Curtis. The dinner fell on the same day as Pat's birthday, and President Mary Mackenzie invited both Pat and Mother to the dinner, and a happy time was had by all.

At this stage I did not realise that serving as the local treasurer could lead to further appointments within our association.

Pat enjoyed working for more than five years as a District Midwife, which was filled with happiness the majority of the time, although tinged with times of sadness, when the mothers needed a lot of help and support.

We worked hard and even when we got home, we had to clean our bags and equipment, launder our white gowns and complete our register of cases. We didn't have a washing machine but every Monday evening we hired a small twin tub to do the bulk of the washing.

In the latter part of 1957, I was asked if I would become a Teaching Midwife, this involved having a pupil midwife living with you for three months.

We had a family discussion, as our house had two bedrooms and a box room. Muriel had the box room, whilst Mother and I shared the back bedroom, so the pupil could have the front bedroom.

I went ahead and received the official letter from the Central Midwives' Board saying the Board had granted my application to be a Teaching District Midwife. I had a telephone extension in the bedroom, which disturbed mother, but she didn't seem to mind and was very good at answering calls if I was already out on a case.

The first pupil midwife was almost twice my age and had a grown up family, not easy to fit in with. It was made more difficult when Mother had a severe angina attack and our GP said she must have complete rest and a bed downstairs for at least two to three weeks. Fortunately, my next pupil midwife was Val Ash, who was the easiest person to fit into our family life and became a life-long friend.

The working day in the life of a district midwife would start depending on how long you had been up during the night and whether it was with one of your own bookings or one of your colleagues, back from her day off. There might be a few telephone calls to make, then you made a list of visits and approximate times, to leave in the window.

The first three days after delivery we visited twice a day, the morning visit lasted about three quarters of an hour, the evening visit half an hour. Then we would visit daily, for about half-an-hour, until the fourteenth day, we also gave care to those discharged from hospital.

On Tuesdays we had an ante-natal clinic at 2pm which could last at least one hour. On top of this we had home ante-natal visits and home condition visits, to see if the house was suitable for a home delivery or if a woman would need a hospital delivery.

I particularly remember one day when myself and my pupil midwife had been up most of the night. There were seven double visits, another twelve or so daily visits, plus an ante-natal clinic. I rarely asked for help, but on this occasion I did, to be flatly refused! I never asked again!

On another occasion, it had been a busy week with disturbed nights and I had the most terrible indigestion, I'd tried all the usual remedies, so on the Saturday I thought I would pop into the Doctors' surgery, only to have two patients in labour!

I dashed between them, one was delivered at Ranmoor at 11am, and I was able to get to Fulwood for the second patient by 12:30pm, in time for the baby to be delivered at 1:30pm. The Doctor came to the second delivery and she took one look at me, and said: "you look awful, when did you last eat?"

Of course, I couldn't remember! Fortunately, it was a nice house, because she shouted down stairs: "please would you make this nurse two poached eggs on toast!" Sometimes we were so tired, we had to take great care driving, but it was a good life.

I must have made a good impression as a teaching midwife, as my supervisor asked if I had thought about undertaking the Midwife Teacher's Diploma. There was one residential course at Kingston-on-Thames and my Supervisor encouraged me to apply and sit the entrance exam. I was successful in gaining a place, starting in the middle of June 1959.

The course lasted for six months and we lived at High Coombe, a large house that had been owned by Lord Liverpool. It was situated in quite extensive grounds which included a gardener's cottage. There were seventeen on the course, fourteen lived in the main house and three in the gardener's cottage. All the bedrooms had been named after a famous artist, I first stayed in Botticelli, which was in the main house, but then one of the students in the cottage had an epileptic fit, and I was asked if I would change rooms. In the cottage, my room was Hals.

It was a very intensive course that was known to normally have less than a fifty per cent pass rate in part one of the exam. Our class didn't do very well, and only three out of seventeen passed part one, and I was not one of the three!

Midwife Teachers Training College.
Pat 3rd from left on back row

When we came home, myself and a friend from Manchester, Vera Turner, went to Northern General Hospital every Thursday afternoon to receive help from Miss Dennis, the Senior Midwifery Tutor. During the week, I put in as much time as possible, practicing answering previous questions. Miss Dennis was an amazing tutor; I always remember one of the comments she made on some written work: "too much to digest."

I felt much better prepared by the time I re-sat the part one exam in May 1960. Out of the twelve of our original group who re-sat the exam, only three more were successful and I was one of the three!

The letter from the Central Midwives' Board stated that I was eligible to enter for part two of the examination to be held on 11th July 1960. The application form had to be returned with an entry fee of four guineas, as soon as possible.

The examinations were held in London at the Central Midwives' Board, they were purely practical and lasted an hour and a half. The building they were held in had previously belonged to Gilbert and Sullivan and I can remember the beautiful woodwork, but engraved above the door of the room we took the exams in were the words:

"Abandon hope all ye that enter here."

In spite of these forebodings, I was successful in passing part two of the Midwife Teacher's Diploma. My friend Vera, did not attempt the examinations again and a year or so later, she emigrated to New Zealand but we have remained pen pals ever since.

I continued working as a district midwife, but I had two pupil midwives attached to me, although they lived in the nurses' home; we were having some alterations done to our house, so it was not convenient to have pupils living with us. In 1961, the post of Assistant Supervisor of Midwives was vacant, I applied and was successful.

For my new post I worked in an office with the Supervisor of Midwives, and had a change of uniform to a grey costume, blouse and tie. I was particularly involved with the student midwives undertaking their District Midwifery Training. We also had to maintain a high standard of practice, with the 50 or so district midwives working in Sheffield, this included record keeping and equipment. At the weekend we took it in turn to be on call from home, we also carried a bleeper in case we had to go out. Muriel and I decided that it would be good to go to an evening class for keep fit, which we enjoyed. Then one evening I tripped over my own feet and fell quite heavily, hurting my right wrist. I went to work the next day but had lost power in my wrist, so during my lunch break I went to the Royal Hospital to have an x-ray which showed a fractured scaphoid! The scaphoid is a small bone on the thumb side of the wrist. The Consultant said I must have a 'pot' on for three months, because if it did not unite it would cause further problems. The plaster went on and it was back to work. My main problem was, being right handed, that my handwriting was terrible, and to keep the plaster looking clean I put Blanco on it!

Towards the end of the three months in plaster I was on call at the weekend when I got a message on the Saturday at 10:30. There was a labour call and they couldn't find a midwife, I tried several numbers to no avail, they were all out on their visits. So my bags were in the car and I went to the house two to three miles away to find the lady in advanced labour. I put a plastic glove over the pot and I successfully delivered the baby, the midwife booked for the case arrived in time to bath the baby!

CENTRAL MIDWIVES BOARD

MIDWIFE TEACHERS DIPLOMA

We hereby Certify

That _Patricia Mary Callis_

state certified midwife No. _139096_ passed

the Midwife Teachers Diploma Examination

in _July 1960._

Arnold Walker
Chairman.

R. J. Fenney
Secretary.

SB

Our cadets

Our St John Cadet Division continued to thrive, with a full programme of activities. Training was important as all cadets, members and officers had to fulfil certain requirements. All ranks had to attend the annual inspection, which was usually held on a Sunday afternoon, unless you had a written excuse. Whether you were an adult or a cadet you had to retake an annual exam in first aid and home nursing. We always used to do this early in the year, to get it out of the way.

For us, preparation for camp was always high on the list.

In 1957 we went to Burnham-on-Sea, Somerset, we had some rain the first two days, then we had brilliant weather. Most years we had a life saver with us, so the cadets were allowed to go swimming, but we still recognised this was a big responsibility, so they were allowed to go in no more than ten at a time, and we would be at the water's edge, doing head counts, and we breathed a sigh of relief when they were all out of the water.

So far we had won several trophies, but the main competition that had evaded us until 1954 was the HL Brown Junior Shield, which we then won for three consecutive years. We also won several other team trophies as well as individual ones. In 1956 our adult team won the Else Trophy in first aid. Competitive work did involve quite a lot of travelling, not only in the Sheffield area, but also in Hull, Ilkeston and Doncaster, to name a few.

We had always encouraged the cadets to attend church parade with the other uniformed organisations. During 1957 we reached two more milestones, the first being getting capes for the cadets to wear, and the second a St John Flag.

Camping at Criccieth

The capes could be bought ready-made, but were very expensive, so we decided to get a similar pattern to the official cape and make them. We went down to the Co-op in Sheffield, bought a pattern and an enormous amount of warm, grey flannel, red cotton material for the lining, reels of cotton and buttons. Our ancient Singer sewing machine worked overtime for several months, producing perfect, warm capes to the delight of all the cadets. The St. John Flag, which would enable us to join with the other organisations' colour parties, were too expensive for us to purchase. We were delighted when the Parents' Association said they would purchase a flag and the leather carrier.

We went to see our Vicar Canon Jordan regarding the dedication of the flag, he was delighted to be asked, particularly as he was due to retire. He suggested an order of service, which we thought was very appropriate, and we agreed to provide service sheets for those attending the service. So Sunday 26th January 1958, the flag was dedicated and blessed in Ecclesall Church before a full congregation and St. John dignitaries. It was a lovely morning.

In 1958 we went by coach to Cricceith, the camp site was a very large field off the main road, and our tents had been delivered in the middle of the field. There were trees all round the perimeter of the site, with plenty of dead wood to collect for the cook's fire and washes. There were numerous shops within walking distance, as well as the sea. The cadets at this camp enjoyed taking it in turn at entertaining, which also involved getting dressed up and it was amazing what they did. We were blessed with good weather and enjoyed a healthy, happy holiday.

Life at Camp.
Silverdale, near Morecambe Bay

During 1958 a flourishing Junior Cadet section was started and at the enrolment ceremony in November, there were ten juniors enrolled into the division. By the end of the year we had four student cadets (who were undertaking the adult certificates), thirty cadets and fourteen juniors.

Every Christmas we had taken presents to elderly people in the Parish and this year we planted 36 bowls of crocuses. These were delivered during the week prior to Christmas, the cadets singing carols at each house.

In 1959 the camp had to be held at Whitsuntide, due to Pat being accepted for her six months Midwifery Teacher's course at the end of June.

This camp was at Silverdale on the West Coast, it was a quiet countryside area, close to Morecambe Bay. Our friend Margaret, who had originally been a member of our Cadet Division, was now a teacher in Sheffield and she decided to start her own Cadet Division in the area where she was teaching, called the Ruskin House Division. We had kept in touch and invited her to come to camp with us, bringing four of her Cadets, all of them were new to camping!

We all mixed in very well and Margaret was known as 'Jem' for Junior Quartermaster, to assist the Quartermaster - 'Quem' Muriel's camp name, Skipper was Pat's camp name and our fourth Officer was Elizabeth Jacques who we called 'Jack'.

The Coach arrived at the Memorial Hall at 7am, and the driver must have wondered how we would get all the kitbags and equipment in the coach. We arrived at the site, after one stop at a wayside cafe, just before mid-day, and after emptying the coach, we sat down and ate our

sandwiches, then changed our uniforms for camp dress.

The camp site, on this occasion, was quite isolated by a beautiful shady lane, the Farm Yard was three fields away. The sea at Silverdale is only a mirage on the horizon, and at high tide it still appeared to be miles away! You could walk across the sands, but there was only a muddy channel running by Jenny Brown's point, not very conducive to swimmers! The village was a fair walk from the site, but it was a perfect camping site, which leant itself to walks, treasure hunts, also some competitive work. So for this camp we thought we would tell our readers more camping details.

All the tents had arrived in the farmyard, about three fields away, so we had to carry the tents, in relays to our field. The cadets worked hard and

soon all the six Bell tents were pitched and the ridge tents. The cook's section, helped by the orderly section, had to turf a large square to make a cooking area and erect the fire shelter. They also, under Quem's supervision, had to prepare and cook the 5:30pm meal.

The wood section had to gather wood and make two wood piles, one for the cooks and one to provide hot water for washing. The health section had to erect the four latrines. The first latrine trench was dug by the farmer, but if got filled in too quickly, we would have to dig the replacement! The water section erected the four wash tents and filled the two dustbins for washing up and night washes.

Then came Skip's nightmare, a 20ft by 14ft marquee had to be erected, this needed everyone to help. The main poles had to have ten campers holding each pole, whilst Skip wielded the enormous mallet. Then all the side poles and detachable curtains had to be firmly erected. Once that is up, Skip can relax!

On the Sunday, two officers and five cadets went to Holy Communion at the parish church. There was an Evensong at 6:30pm so we all walked through the woods to the church where we were met with a great welcome from the Vicar and the congregation, we were invited to a coffee morning later in the week.

The locals proudly told us that there were over 50 public footpaths, and the farmers didn't mind you crossing their fields. After the hectic two days and the long walk, we were all ready for bed, and the nightly ritual commenced: hot cocoa, washes and, when all were in bed, we sang Taps to complete the day.

For those who do not know this, the words are:-
Day is done, Gone the sun From the sea From the hills From the sky,
All is well, safely rest God is nigh.

On the Tuesday, unbeknown to the cadets, we had a mock first aid rescue, the highlight of camp! Everything was normal, Jem and two cadets from the orderly section went shopping for stores whilst Quem arranged the 'accident' at the base of a tree. It was so realistic, some passers by thought it was real!

Quem sent the cadet with her back to camp for help. Skipper went with the team, who thought it was a genuine accident, until they saw the mock blood on the patient's forehead. One member kept the other

campers from the scene, whilst the patient was treated, and it was with great relief to the others when they realized an ambulance was not required.

On the last night of a camp it was always traditional to have a camp fire and invite the local friends we had made. We would all sit around the campfire and the evening started with the Officers and each section doing a short sketch. One of the Officers usually wrote a camp song, mentioning any particular incidents which had occurred during the week, causing lots of laughter and a few red faces. Then we would sing all the favourite camps songs: She'll Be Coming Round the Mountain, There are White Tents on the Hillside, There's a Long, Long Worm a Crawling, We are the Red Men, Eliza Jane and many more. We would also serve cocoa and biscuits to the visitors and cadets (visitors were asked to bring a beaker with them). Then we might sing Knights of St John, finishing the evening with Taps.

When it comes to striking camp, campers always hope for fine weather, so that all the tents and equipment are dry for packing. On this occasion the weather was brilliant. Our journey home was relatively short, so the coach was booked for 5pm and we had ample time to have a cooked lunch, prepare sandwiches for tea on the coach and ensure everything was ready for the Carrier to collect. Then we changed into our uniforms, and made sure all our kitbags and equipment were ready for the coach's arrival.

Our last job was to make sure that the field was left in almost the same condition as it was on arrival, with particular attention to the replacement of turfs in the fire places, ensuring they had been well watered. Our motto was to leave nothing but our thanks.

One good tradition we had at all camps was that each cadet brought a cake in a tin and we had some super cakes, which lasted us the week!

The 1960s were very busy, both for St John activities also our own personal activities, so we will start with the cadets. The 1960 camp was in August at Lligwy Bay, Anglesey. It was a memorable camp as one of the cadets developed chicken pox. Fortunately, she wasn't ill with it, just itchy, which was relieved with calamine lotion, and none of the other cadets had any symptoms.

The weather was not very kind, although it was quite warm, and we remember on the last night, when it was pouring with rain, taking the cocoa round to the tents in our swimming costumes!

So much happens in a youth organisation, we could fill many books with stories, but much of it is repetitive, so we will continue to cover the years up to 1965 by indicating the regular events, and make mention of anything special.

To obtain the Grand Prior Badge, the cadets had to study the Knowledge of the Order of St. John, and pass an exam. As well as the first aid and home nursing exams, they also had to study and pass exams on subjects such as childcare, firefighting, cookery, animal care, hygiene, toy making and clerical ability.

In 1960 the Parents' Association organised a visit to St John's Gate, Clerkenwell, where they were able to see some of the historical artefacts, which are kept at the headquarters. This was a great help to the cadets when they were taking the Knowledge of the Order exam, it was a very happy day.

Members of the Ecclesall Cadet Nursing Corps. are justly proud of the trophies they won the previous year. Here we see the girls admiring them at their H.Q. The Ecclesall Church hall. The trophies include the H.L. Brown Junior Shield: the Ledger Individual trophy, the Beverly Rose Bowl; the Norton Cup; The Else trophy and Holland Cup.

Over the years, many cadets worked hard to gain the Grand Prior Badge and although they could not all have Princess Margaret to present it, they would be given out by a local dignitary at a special event, such as Sheffield's Mistress Cutler.

Our division was honoured by one of the cadets being chosen to represent the area in the Guard of Honour, at the wedding of Her Royal Highness Princess Margaret.

In 1960 our president, Miss Barraclough, resigned due to ill health, she had been a great support and was sadly missed. In the same year, our new Vicar and his wife arrived and very quickly found people in the parish who would benefit from a visit particularly at Christmas. Each year we had a list of at least sixty homes where the residents would welcome a visit and a present.

They also encouraged at the Harvest Festival, donations of tinned food, which could be given out at Christmas. It took us about a week to wrap the

Visit to London

parcels and a week to deliver them, and the cadets came to help, usually ten to twenty each night. If it was raining the numbers dwindled! One year, there was a flu outbreak and on the last night of deliveries we had one stalwart who had turned up every night, plus the two of us, but all the parcels were delivered!

In 1961, the Vicar's wife, Alison became our Division's new, 'hands on' President.

The cadets also performed concerts, hosted jumble sales, held coffee mornings in the church entrance, helped at the church garden parties, gave first aid demonstrations and a whole host of other activities. All the activities fitted in with our Code of Chivalry: "for the service of mankind." The Parents' Association supported us at every event.

Competitive work took a lot of time and energy, plus of course providing transport. We always encouraged the cadets to enter, as we considered it would hold them in good stead in later years to show a competitive streak. In one regional competition we gained the home

nursing trophy and finished just two points off winning the competition, which would have taken us to London.

The cadets were also competitive at swimming competitions which many entered winning many prizes. In 1964 we were the overall winners, gaining the swimming trophy.

Looking back we have always been competitive, if you want to succeed you must always keep on trying and you will succeed.

To take the cadets' activities up to 1965 we have to briefly mention four more camps. In 1961 we went by coach to Rhownair, Towyn, on the coast of Mid Wales. One cadet was prone to travel sickness, so Skipper took her and our poodle - Ricky, by car and had no problems with her.

Trip up the mountain in Wales

This wasn't the same on the coach, as they were approaching Buxton, the first cadet felt sick, then another and another; to cut a long story short, when they arrived at the camp site, the coach floor had to be swilled with Dettol and a sweeping brush. All those who were sick had drank copious amount of orange juice with their breakfast!

The site was delightful and the weather was fine and warm. On the return journey, orange juice was banned, the coach arrived home clean.

The 1962 camp was held in August at Burnham-on-Sea. We had a damp start, but it latterly improved. The highlight of the camp was a visit to Cheddar Gorge.

In 1963 we went to Roewen, Conway, North Wales. The coach had a problem negotiating a tight bend in Conway, requiring Skipper's assistance to direct the traffic! The driver had the start of a migraine attack, so he stayed the night, sleeping in the coach. It was a lovely camp with brilliant weather.

Visit to Cheddar Gorge

We had three sets of twins at the 1964 Camp in Tre-Arddur Bay, Anglesey. One of one set of twins had been blind from birth, her twin had been to camp previously and told her about it, and she decided to try it. She found certain aspects more difficult, but it was good to see how the other cadets rallied round helping her.

In August 1965 we went to Grange Over Sands, it was a large site, surrounded by trees, but there were walks close to the site. Although there were plenty of trees, there was very little wood on the ground to pick up. So Skip took the big axe and attacked an area of dead wood, unfortunately disturbing a wasps' nest! She shouted all to move away quickly, but she had many stings! The camp nurse Val Ash and Quem got the bicarbonate of soda, mixed it to a paste and bandaged it over the stings, this together with calamine lotion and anti-histamine tablets worked wonders. The rest of the week was enjoyable.

Ass. Quem, Skip, Camp Nurse, Quem

Family events

We will continue with our own events in the 1960s, firstly mentioning the major repair work to our church. The width of the nave at All Saints, Ecclesall, was comparable to the width of a Cathedral, and the roof required stainless steel supports, so the whole area had to be isolated.

The transepts were filled with extra seats, so that services continued as usual. All this was expensive and the Vicar and his wife Alison were full of ideas to raise money, including getting to know the right people who could help.

The Cutlers' Hall was booked for a Stewardship Campaign, which included a meal. The church wardens sent out invitations to the entire Ecclesall Parish population. The Cutlers' Hall was a fine building to welcome the large number who responded and the money started to roll in, the evening was a resounding success!

The PCC was rather large, sometimes thirty or forty attending, Muriel was on the PCC representing the Kindergarten Sunday school and she found the meetings lively and enjoyable. The next project on the agenda was the need to improve and enlarge the Memorial Rooms. Plans were drawn up for the PCC to approve, which showed a large hall with a stage that linked to the existing halls, plus a new entrance, with cloakroom and toilet facilities. This would be built on the large area of land belonging to the church.

The church membership grew with all the activities, and before long the work was completed and the new halls being used, which indicated it was required in a growing community.

Stone Henge - when the public could walk around

The Vicar and his wife lived in Germany between 1950 and 1953, and in 1946 he had been a member of a Bishop's Churchmen's delegation to all the churches in Germany. They made many friends who they kept in touch with. It was his wish to have a morning service between Germany and England, which was organised by the BBC television service and Nordwestdeutsche Rundfunk, a German broadcasting service.

On Sunday 26th February 1961 we had a live morning service between All Saints, Ecclesall, and the Kreuzkirche, Wolfsburg, Germany from 10:15am to 11am. Our church was full. The only practice we had was to sing the hymns through once, then we were live, and it went out without hitch! We still have a copy of the service and the sermon.

Alison Hanson, the Vicar's wife, was an excellent flower arranger who brought new ideas for Advent from Germany. One of ideas was to make an advent crown, and soon many churches started following suit. We still make one every year for the church we belong to, although Alison's advent crown is hard to match.

We decided in 1962 to explore further afield for our holiday. We both put in for the same two weeks break and started planning to go to Cornwall, making a booking for eleven days full board at the Chypons Hotel at Newlyn, near Penzance. Due to the long journey we arranged to

At Land's End on our 1962 visit to Cornwall

LAND'S END CAR PARK

N? 25516

CHARGE 1/-

Vehicles may be parked here on condition it is agreed that neither the proprietors nor their servants shall be liable for loss of or damage to any vehicle or its accessories or contents however caused while so parked.

stay overnight on the way down at Burnham-on-Sea. We planned the route carefully with an Ordinance Survey map, looking for all the historic places of interest.

We started our holiday on the Sunday, first taking Ricky, our small black poodle, for a walk in the woods, then we were on our way. We stopped to eat our sandwiches near Kidderminster, before joining the A38, the main road to the west - there were no motorways, and less traffic in 1962!

We arrived at the hotel in Burnham-on-Sea at 6pm, ready for dinner, then we went for a walk before bed. Mother was a good traveller and she enjoyed every minute of the journey, it was something new to her.

By 9:30am the following day were on our way, making a short detour to visit Clovelly, where we parked the car and walked down to the delightful, pretty village. Many years later we attempted to visit this area again, as we had such happy memories, but it was ruined with an enormous entrance building where you had to pay to visit. We rejoined the A39 then the A30 road, arriving at the Chypons Hotel at 5:30pm. The hotel was at the top of a hill, with wonderful views of the sea and the busy fishing harbour of Newlyn with its quaint cottages.

On the first day we explored Penzance's shops and the pottery, stopping to have coffee. Mother decided she had walked far enough and sat on the sands whilst we took Ricky to Mousehole, a quaint village with just one road and no footpaths, then we all went back to the hotel for lunch. The food was excellent, particularly the banana splits and the fresh strawberries with local ice cream.

Whilst Mother rested in the hotel, we went to Lamora Cove. We parked the car then walked with Ricky on a quiet path through the woods, with the sun shining through the trees. After dinner, a further short walk before we retired to our rooms, to be ready for an early start the next day, when we went to the jetty to embark on the R.M.V. Scillonian for our visit to the Scilly Isles. It was a calm sea, the sun was shining and there was only a slight breeze. It was 40 miles to the Isles and took three hours, once we had left Land's End there was more of a swell, but we three and Ricky were fine and enjoyed it, remaining on the deck for the journey. As we passed Longships Lighthouse and Wolfrock we had reached half way.

On arrival at St. Mary's we found seats, so we could enjoy the packed lunch we had brought from the hotel overlooking the blue sea and warm sands. Mother decided the deck chair was comfortable and she was enjoying the views and the people passing by. We took Ricky on a long walk and visited the church, before buying ice creams for all of us. The boat sailed at 4:30pm, the Scillonian was the lifeline for everything the locals required, so there was always a lot of unloading and loading taking place at both ends. It was a very smooth return crossing, arriving back at 7:45pm for a late dinner, it had been a wonderful day.

The following day, Mother was feeling tired and suffering from too much sun, so we had three quiet days with Mother staying in her room until lunch. We went to Marazian, taking Ricky over the causeway to St Michael's Mount, just coming back over the causeway before the tide covered it. After lunch, we all went to Land's End where we saw the First and Last House and had our photos taken with the distance to Sheffield in miles on it. Land's End has changed over the years, for example the car park fee was one shilling.

On the next quiet day, with mother staying in until lunch, we went to Penzance to get the car washed and vacuumed, then after lunch we went to the local church fete, before returning to the hotel for Mother and going to the Admiral Benbows for afternoon tea.

On the Sunday, Mother's angina was playing up, so we asked the doctor to call. He came at 4pm and left a prescription which Pat took in the car to Sennen for the tablets, but at the bottom of the hill the car conked out, we called the AA and it was a carburettor problem, which was soon sorted out and Mother's tablets were obtained.

We went a short run in the cool of the evening to St Ives, but it was very busy so we went on to Carbis Bay, which was lovely and Ricky was able to have a good run.

The following day, Mother was feeling much better, so we were able to take her a ride to a very pretty cove nearby. We took a camp bed with us, so she was able to relax in the sea air, whilst we were able to take Ricky for a long walk. The doctor called again just before dinner and was very pleased with Mother's improvement.

After dinner the two of us went to the Minack Theatre, Porthcono, which is a delightful outdoor theatre. We saw the play 'A Penny for a Song' by John Whiting, performed by The Worcester College Buskins, Oxford. It was an amazing production, one actor spent the entire performance high up on a seat fastened to a rock! It was a lovely fine evening and the play finished at 10:30pm, arriving back at the hotel at 11:15pm.

The next day we went to St Just then on to Cape Cornwall and Maldron, where we tried to find the wishing well, but were told it had caved in, the previous week. In the afternoon we took Mother to the hairdressers in Penzance whilst we went to Prussia Cove - a very pretty cove. The tide was nearly in so we walked a little way, then sat on the rocks for a while before returning to Penzance. After dinner we walked to see the Baptistery where John Wesley had preached, it was a beautiful evening.

Our last day was the first dull day, so we watched the Scillonian leave Penzance, looked at the shops then drove to Hale and Hell's Mouth, where the sea was quite rough and we only had a short walk as it was very windy. The weather improved in the afternoon so we went to Logan Rock to admire the wonderful views and on to Portgwarra - another lovely cove. Ricky, who was a good swimmer, ran over the rocks and then jumped into the sea, swimming back to us. Then, we went back to our hotel to pack our cases, ready for an early start the following morning.

In the morning we took Ricky down to the quay and watched the unloading of the fish, then it was back for breakfast and with the car packed we were on our way home at 8:45am, with many happy memories of our visit to Cornwall.

Mother often talked about Canada and America, saying she would like to visit friends and relatives, whom we corresponded with frequently, especially the sister of her ex-fiancée Gordon, who was killed at Passchendaele. She had lived there for about five years, coming home during World War One.

Mother had contributed to an insurance policy, this matured in 1963 and we insisted that she should spend it on herself and go to Canada and America for two months, and in a wild moment, Mother said yes!

She had a passport, so off we went to Cooks to arrange a passage on the Queen Mary in May, returning on the Queen Elizabeth in July. Mother had to have a smallpox vaccination prior to going to Liverpool to obtain a visa.

Although Mother was very excited to be going away, there was a degree of apprehension, after all it was a long voyage on her own. We both arranged to take her to Southampton, booking in at a hotel. One of the representatives Pat had met at work knew the staff on the Queen Mary, and

Photographed on board.RMS. QUEEN ELIZABETH.

when we arrived on the liner, Mother's cabin had been upgraded and there were flowers inside, which was a lovely surprise. We waited on the quay, which was an excitement in itself with the band playing all the traditional naval music.

It was a relief when we received Mother's postcard from Cherbourg, France, and she sounded quite settled. Further letters showed that the voyage had been extremely rough, in the middle of one night she decided to dress and one morning she had been the only one to go in for breakfast!

When they landed in New York she then took a Greyhound bus 600miles to Cleveland, Ohio, she mentioned that she was not well, so we decided to telephone her and she was feeling much better. By the beginning of June she was able to visit her friend in Toronto and a cousin in Ottawa, Canada, before returning to Cleveland, Ohio.

All too soon it was time for Mother to return to New York, accompanied by her cousin and her husband. The return journey on the Queen Elizabeth was much calmer and everyone was very friendly. We were both at Southampton to meet Mother after her epic journey, looking fit.

Once in a lifetime

We had mentioned that the 1960s were a busy time, and this now continues with Pat applying for a Travel Scholarship. The initial information was published in the Midwives' Chronicle in the latter part of 1963 by the British Commonwealth Nurses War Memorial Fund, so I decided to write a letter expressing my interest.

On the 14th January 1964 I received a reply telling me I was one of the candidates chosen to write an essay, of no more than 2,500 words, on: 'How would you design a programme of basic training which would prepare nurses to meet the nursing needs of the community?'

The essay needed to reach their office by 11th February, so I had to put my skates on! After much toil and sweat, I was satisfied with my essay and sent it off. A further letter on 17th March informed me that I was one of the candidates called for interview on 7th April at 3pm, at Dorset House, Stamford Street, and would I confirm that I would be able to attend.

The next letter came on 14th April telling me that I had been awarded a Permanent Fund Scholarship for 1964/1965, requesting a photograph of myself and a medical certificate. At this stage I could only tell my immediate family until the official announcements were made in August.

Meanwhile I had to send my proposed itinerary to be approved by the Scholarship Committee, this was approved on the 14th June and they would contact the International Confederation of Midwives (ICM) at the Royal College of Midwives, who would arrange the official contacts in each country. One of the scholarship winners, Miss Chivers, was also planning to go to Paris and we were able to team up. The presentation of certificates took place on November 17th at the Royal College of Midwives 3:30pm. The certificates were presented by Viscountess Davidson (Baroness Northchurch).

From then onwards into 1965 I had frequent letters from Miss Bayes (ICM Secretary) with detailed information about my tour, including contacts and accommodation, starting in France and travelling to Belgium, Holland, Germany, Denmark, Sweden, Finland and Norway. This would be the first time I had been abroad.

My study tour was to run between the 15th March 1965 and 11th June 1965. The scholarship was for £500 and this was duly transferred to me so I was able to sort out travellers cheques. It was a very busy time, but before I left England I had to visit my 95-year-old Grandmother in Blackpool, whose health was failing; Mother, Muriel and I went at the beginning of March.

Trip on the Seine

My scholarship was to study the maternity services in the various countries. In particular, I was interested in the psychoprophylactic method of preparing for childbirth, which was being practised in Paris under the direction of Dr Hersillie. A method I was later to teach to hundreds of mothers and midwives.

Although my programme during the three months kept me

very busy, I tried to see as much of the countries as possible, making use of the weekends. I will only mention small interesting stories of the midwifery part of my tour and concentrate more on the countries, which will make easier reading.

It was the first time I had flown! So here I was at Manchester Airport, saying goodbye to Mother, Muriel and Ricky for three months. My flight was from Ringway to Orly Airport by Air France Caravelle. One can really appreciate the beauty of the green fields of England when you see the country from a plane!

Gradually the countryside disappeared from sight as the plane increased its height and flew above a heavy blanket of fog. The next sight of land was as we crossed into France, the area was densely populated, with very little countryside until we were near Paris, where there were many rivers, reservoirs and forests. Then the River Seine came into sight with all the bridges and boats and we were soon drifting in to land at Orly. This large, modern airport was buzzing with people, but there was little formality - only a passport check and then on to collect the luggage.

The bus was waiting to take us to the air terminal in Paris, where I took a taxi to the hotel on Rue St. Maur. It was a poor area, but close to the Centre de Sante des Métallurgistes, and the Maternity unit. The hotel was a small bed and breakfast, my bedroom had above the bed a picture of a nude female! I met Muriel Chivers with whom I was spending the first week with. The French midwives spoke very little English and we spoke very little French! In the end, if we wanted to ask a question, I would ask it in 'French' and Muriel Chivers would write the answer in English; that sounds a bit complicated but it did help.

We were also fortunate to meet a Danish midwife - Charlotte - who was on the same course and spoke good English. The week passed all too quickly, and we had thoroughly enjoyed the experience, including seeing two mothers deliver their babies using this method of preparation - they both said their delivery had been sans douleur (without pain).

On the Friday night, one of the French midwifes invited us to go to a night club in Montmartre, close to Sacré-Coeur. It was very crowded and noisy, so we had a drink and stayed about an hour, realising that we were being used, as our host was having boyfriend problems! At least we saw Sacré-Coeur floodlit and a bit of Parisian nightlife.

On the Saturday, Muriel Chivers left to catch the plane back to England as her scholarship was going to the USA, so we said goodbye and wished each other an enjoyable three months. I then went for a trip on the River Seine and found out where the English church was situated. I went to church on the Sunday, then Charlotte met me. We had a meal on the Champs-Élysées, followed by visiting the Arc de Triomphe, here we saw the Eternal Flame then went by the lift to the top where we could walk outside to view Paris in front of us, the views were amazing. Then we walked to the Eiffel Tower, followed by taking the metro to Notre Dame and walking down the boulevard with the stalls displayed. We came across a shop selling hot waffles which were delicious. It was then time to return to the hotel and pack my suitcase for leaving the next day. Charlotte came to the station with me, we hoped to meet her again in Sweden, her boyfriend was living there and she was working there.

The train took me on to Brussels, where I stayed in hospital accommodation. Fortunately, I had time to settle in and have a quick walk round Brussels, because that was the only opportunity I had. The following day I travelled to a hospital in Charleroi, a mining town south of Brussels, then to Namur, a rural area, staying overnight in private hospitals. Altogether I visited six private hospitals and two government hospitals, none of the hospitals had baths or showers. The private hospitals were run by the Catholic Sisters who worked very long hours, whilst the government hospitals were overcrowded and there was a shortage of midwives. The last two days in Belgium were spent in Brussels, and I was able to get a picture of Edith Cavell, a British nurse who had been the Matron at the Nurses' Training Institute in Brussels, and was shot by the Germans in 1915 for helping allied soldiers escape over the Dutch frontier. Belgium was a different country to France, I noticed many ladies, all dressed in black and this was because they had been widowed, but there were so many. I also noticed that beer was widely drank openly by youngsters - this was in

Charleroi Clinique

1965, so I am sure there will have been many changes.

After Belgium I went by train to Holland, where I stayed for two weeks, my headquarters being The Hague. During the two weeks I travelled quite a distance, to Rotterdam, Utrecht, 's-Hertogenbosch and Stein, in the Province of Limburg, staying overnight in the latter two places due to them being so distant.

The Hague is the administrative centre for health services – the Dutch system is rather complex, founded on the close co-operation between the National, Local and Provincial authorities and private agencies. Amongst the private agencies, the Cross Association operated throughout the country - the white and yellow Cross for Roman Catholics, the orange and green for Protestants, the green Cross was not associated with religion, although in the south of Holland, green was Roman Catholic.

I had my 33rd birthday whilst I was in The Hague, so in the evening I treated myself to a very special ice cream sundae, then I went to the

cinema to watch My Fair Lady, which was lovely, I was humming the tunes for days. At the weekend I saw as much as I could of this fascinating country, high on the list was Rotterdam, which was the second largest port.

Our vicar, Dick Hanson, had given me an introduction to the Padre for the Missions to Seamen, so on the Sunday I went to the service there, then I was taken on the boat that goes round the docks inviting the sailors to visit the Mission to Seamens in the harbour. I went to the villages of Volendam and Marken, where the villagers wore traditional costumes and lived in quaint houses. Also on the list of must-visit destinations was Kerkenhoph, the beautiful gardens, and the pleasures of Amsterdam.

The furthest I travelled was to Stein, and I had get up at 5:30am, to have breakfast and catch the 7:03am train to visit a midwife who lived with her parents. I spent two pleasant days at a nearby hotel for bed and breakfast, and accompanied the midwife on her visits. The midwife's mother was a good cook and provided the other meals, so I had some real Dutch food which was very good. They ate a lot of yoghurt, which was new to me, but I soon developed a taste.

I spent two days in Utrecht at De Ooiemaar - The Stork - which was a large Georgian type mansion which catered for up to 30 mothers at a time. 600 babies were delivered a year, as well as 100 home deliveries. They wanted me to stay the night, but I hadn't come prepared and something told me to go back to The Hague, when I returned there was a letter waiting for me saying that Granny had died, it was good that we had taken the time to visit her before I left for my travels.

There was so much to see in Holland, but before I left I wanted to see Madurodam, a miniature town, it was marvellous. The planes went up and down the runway, the ships sail, one of them is launched from a dry dock. Cars moved, water wheels turned, it is so clever and I only had half an hour to take it all in! I had spent a lovely, interesting two weeks in Holland.

My next country was Germany, where I spent only four days. The train took me to Cologne, where I saw the famous 14th century Cathedral before continuing to Wuppertal, where I stayed at a large, new maternity hospital. The staff showed me round, but I got the impression that I was

only shown what they wanted me to see. I had an upset stomach, but soldiered on.

In the afternoon a couple from the hospital took me to a zoo, which was quite famous and in lovely grounds. Then in the evening they took me to the Opera House to see The Bartered Bride, which I enjoyed very much. In the interval they gave me some Indian brandy to settle my stomach. My hosts were so friendly and I wasn't allowed to pay for anything, although we did have some language problems.

The next day I took the 6:50am train to Hamburg, to be met by the midwife, who should have arranged my programme. She apologised profusely and told me it was impossible for her, as a midwife, to do this - the midwives had a low status and there was a great deal of friction between the Doctors and the Midwives. Arrangements had been made for me to stay for two nights with a delightful German family - Mr and Mrs Peterson and their children, aged seven and two. Mrs Peterson completed her general and midwifery training in England and her husband taught English and History at the High School. What a relief, we had so much to talk about, and through Mrs Peterson's efforts I was able to visit a private maternity home and a maternity hospital. I also heard about the problems of the domiciliary midwives. I left Germany the following day disappointed that there were so many problems.

The journey from Hamburg to Denmark started by train, then to cross the water between the two countries, the train went on a boat, before continuing to Copenhagen. The Danes on the journey were very friendly and spoke good English.

When I arrived at the hotel I wondered where I was going, but then realised many of the hotels were above shops or offices. I had a pleasant room with a wash basin, and a toilet and bathroom next door. I had instructions to ring a Mrs Vonsild at her clinic, she arranged to pick me up at 7pm, and brought with her a bunch of anemones for me. From her car she pointed out places of interest, then we had a meal at the station restaurant. The Danish know how to cook; we had a meat based soup into which they beat an egg, then salmon cooked in a thin batter with asparagus tips, crisps, potatoes, a tomato sauce and shrimps, washed down with a Tuborg lager.

Mrs Vonsild's mother owned a private clinic, where she worked, she gave me the instructions of the hospitals and clinics I would be visiting, and the district midwife I would meet. She had left plenty of time for sight seeing, and there was so many interesting places.

On the Sunday I went to St. Albans Church for morning service, then walked to see where the 'little mermaid' is, then to the Citadel, which was like a barracks. Near the church is The Gefion Fountain, a marvellous fountain where water comes steaming from the beasts' nostrils. There are many palaces, the main one being the Christiansborg Palace, a beautiful building where all the official visitors, Kings, Queens, Presidents and Ambassadors are received. To go round the palace you have to put felt overshoes on - to protect the floors, what a beautiful palace.

Underneath the building are the ruins of Absalon's old palace, including two wells- one has pure water in it but the other was poisoned by enemies hundreds of years ago and has never been purified. Rosenborg Palace stores the Crown Jewels and one of the Coronation Thrones, in front of the throne are three, solid silver lions, each at least three feet in height, plus a clock, that has figures which move round when it strikes. In the centre of Copenhagen there is a large statue of Hans Anderson.

One last castle I visited in Elsinore was Kronborg, where Hamlet has been performed. Keeping guard is the statue of Ogier the Dane - it is said that if Denmark is attacked he will wake up and fight!

It is a lovely country to visit, and everyone is so friendly. Just before I left, I met a lady from Israel who was on a Scholarship from World Health to study hospital buildings, she was going to Sweden, so I said I would look out for her.

I made my way to Sweden by train and boat, which took about five and a half hours. I had been booked in at a hotel in Goteborg for four nights, which included a weekend, so it left a very short time.

On the Monday I met the Senior Tutor at the hospital and spent the two days with her, she was very anxious for me to meet the Professor who

"...but the best of all, she said, was to lie in the moonlight on a sandbar in the calm sea and look at the great city near the coast, where the lights twinkled like hundreds of stars." FROM HANS CHRISTIAN ANDERSEN'S FAIRY TALE

The Little Mermaid

Oiger The Dane

Hilsen fra KRONBORG

111

invented the Vacuum Extractor - an alternative to forceps. He was giving a lecture, to which I went, he spoke part of the lecture in English for my benefit, it was very interesting.

Following this short visit, I took the six-hour train journey to Stockholm, enjoying a meal and meeting some friendly people who pointed out a small white church, which was typical of Sweden. The terrain was quite rocky, with wooden houses nestling between the rocks, but later it flattened out with pine trees and stretches of water.

I was met at Stockholm station by the President of the Swedish Midwives' Association who took me to the hotel, which was for women only, and told me about my programme. I would have guides to show me round Stockholm too - Charlotte, whom I met in Paris and Gunilla, another midwife - everyone was so friendly. One night, after spending the day at the hospital, the midwife invited me to her home, we had a great time shelling shrimps, which were very tasty with toast, white wine, cheese, peaches and coffee.

Another night I had a delicious meal with Gunilla and her parents. On 30th April it was Walpurgis night - which signifies the end of spring. I was taken to Skansen Park, where there was dancing in national costume and a procession carrying a special garland on a pole. For the men, barrels were suspended on a frame and, either on horseback or running, they had to knock them down. As well as the bonfires, there was an amazing fireworks display. Another day I went on a river trip, watched the Changing of the Guards, and the old part of Stockholm with very narrow streets.

A Saturday outing was to Uppsala, where we went round the University, Cathedral, gardens and the castle. In Old Uppsala there are three mounds believed to be the burial ground of three Vikings. We had a meal in a very old restaurant where you drink Viking mead out of a horn. On the Sunday Charlotte and boyfriend Gustaf came by car, we went to one of the 4,000 islands in Sweden, to visit the Carl Milles gardens. He was a sculptor who died in 1955, the gardens had many bronze statues, all amazing. One depicted man on God's hand. Our fantastic day was completed with a meal at Gustaf's parents home, a beautiful, detached house in large grounds. The meal was superb, I felt like a Queen! One of their friends drove me back to my hotel at 11pm!

My hectic, enjoyable time in Stockholm was drawing to a close but I was told I could not leave without visiting the City Hall, it was opened in 1923. There is a Golden room, where the walls and ceiling are in 18 carat gold mosaic! You are able to go so far up the tower by a lift, then you go round winding passages to get to the top, there are 365 steps! On one of the floors there is a statue, about 20 ft. high, of the man who found Stockholm. The view from the tower was well worth going up all the steps.

It was time then to board the ship, to sail overnight to Turku in Finland, I had a first class ticket in berth 33, a nice little cabin with a porthole. The crossing was slow because the ship has to negotiate so many islands, varying in size, some had summer houses.

Dinner was served at 6:40pm and I had six gentlemen to keep me company at our table. The table where you helped yourself was loaded with food, fish dishes, chicken, moulds, mayonnaise, mixed vegetables, potatoes, beetroot, onions, tomatoes, cucumber, lettuce to start with, then we were served with veal cutlets and puree potatoes followed by rhubarb and whipped cream. The gentleman next to me didn't think I had enough whipped cream so added an extra pile!

Then we went upstairs for coffee and it was announced that we would arrive in Turku at 8am and the train to Helsinki would leave at 8:45am. The clocks had been moved on one hour during the night. The scenery is beautiful, it is known as the 1,000 islands. I did not sleep very well as it was rather noisy, but dosed off eventually. There was so much to see, so I was up at 6:00am and we landed on time.

On arrival in Helsinki, I went to the Midwives' Headquarters, where there was a room for visitors to stay. In Finland you are entertained continuously - the story goes that the visitor leaves exhausted whilst the Finns prepare for the next guest!

During my two weeks in Finland I did not have a chance to see much of Helsinki, other than from out of a car window. I travelled each day in a large chauffeur driven car, but on the first day the car wouldn't start and this poor, little man tried blowing the petrol tubes out, cleaning the carburettor, and after three attempts, he won, and we had no further trouble.

All the babies are delivered in hospital, and the midwives undertake the ante-natal and post-natal care and the clinics. A midwife took me to two visits, then we had a snack at a cafeteria in a pleasant district called Tapiola, the views were marvellous. We drove round an area they called West End where there were very modern, large houses. We returned to the clinic until it finished at 5.30pm, then returned to the headquarters.

The Supervisors from the different Communes came for a meeting at their headquarters and in the evening invited me to go to a restaurant, and how they enjoyed their drink! I think it was Schnapps, I was brought a glass and it was only when I was feeling a bit wobbly that I realized they had been topping up my drink!

For my second week I took an overnight train to Jyvaskyla, it was very noisy trying to sleep on the train and there were two other people in the cabin! I was met by one of the Supervisors at the station at about 7am and she took me to a similar type of Headquarters as in Helsinki.

My programme was non-stop! I also had reporters queuing up to interview me. In each Commune I visited the day started off with the

Jyvaskyla

midwives in that area congregated in one of the houses, and there was a spread of food, each had contributed some food and they were quite intent that I should sample everything!

To get to Saarijarvi we had a bus journey of over one and a half hours, some roads were muddy due to the severe winters, the scenery was picturesque with lakes and trees. Most cottages are painted red so they can be distinguished in the snow.

One of the staff with a car took us to a place called Ahvenlampi, where there is a big lake. In the summer it is a camping ground with some permanent buildings. All round the lake are numerous sauna houses. They took me a different way back past a cemetery and a modern chapel.

At the Health Centre, I met the Communal Doctor, who showed me round a small hospital with 38 beds, 11 of which were maternity beds, it was interesting and enjoyable. Then we went to a restaurant where a lovely meal awaited us. They sure know how to cook. The bus that took us back to Jyvaskyla was also the post bus and stopped at all the post boxes to collect the mail.

On Sunday my host came at 11:40am to take me to a hotel for lunch and she was anxious for me to meet an American man who was teaching them English, he was a strange man in a nice sort of way, a bit eccentric and never stopped talking! We left at 2pm and walked back to the flat. At 3pm another friend came in her car, we first went to a TB Sanatorium they wanted me to see as they had a flat roof you can walk on and have a marvellous view, we also had a quick look round. Then we went to a ski jump, the road twisted and was very steep. At the top is this enormous tower, it had been opened to the public the previous Sunday at noon and at 4pm the lift broke down! Not to be outdone I climbed to the top, 350 steps to be rewarded with a superb view!

We then had a sauna appointment, the sauna house was about 12 yards from the edge of the lake. There was a hot room which is stoked up with pine wood, the temperature went up to eighty degrees centigrade and when your skin feels tacky then it runs with water, you rush out to the lake and have a swim, the water was 10 degrees C. I ducked quickly and dashed back! Then you had to wash using a soft brush, have warm followed by cold water poured over you, then retire to the summer house for a rub down, cover with a warm wrap, drink pineapple juice, relax for half an hour, then get dressed. All very interesting!

The following day we went to Jamsa, after we had visited the Health Centre, we walked to a nearby restaurant where we were entertained to dinner by the Director of the Commune. I was the first English visitor, the flag on the table was the stars and stripes instead of the Union Jack!

After lunch we were taken to see the largest newspaper manufacturing mill in the world, it was most interesting, seeing the wood floating down the river to the mill. We went to a house on the factory estate, for cream puffs, coffee and liqueurs. Then I was presented with a beautiful book from the Director and Midwives, with pictures of the area.

I kept telling my hosts in Jyvaskyla that I must visit the travel bureau at 9am, two days before I was due to leave. I hurried to the bureau before our daytrip, told them the details, and was told I had to return the following day.

To reach my next destination, I had to reach Oulu by 4:20pm to get the train to Narvik. The Public Health Nurse Supervisor said she would drive me the 340 kilometres, which included some mud tracks, to Oulu, as she had a visit in that direction.

We had a safe journey to Oulu with twenty minutes to spare, I was so grateful I gave the nurse the Finnish money I had left towards the petrol. Fortunately I had sent one of my suitcases from Helsinki to Oslo for me to pick up when I arrived there, but I still had a fair amount to carry!

Continuing my epic journey I boarded the train to Tonio, from there I took a five minute train journey to Harpanda, a Finnish/Swedish border town, the clocks had to be moved back an hour. From Harpanda I took the train to Boden, arriving at 10:56pm. The next train north wasn't until 2:43am, and I had to wait in bitterly cold temperatures, walking round the station until the station master opened the waiting room, which was not comfy but a little warmer.

I was soon joined by a couple of drunks, so decided to take a walk, as it was daylight. My walk was cut short when I was whistled by a man who began to follow me, fortunately there were some men working on the station, so I walked up to where they were and the man went.

Eventually the train arrived and I just had one more change at 6:20am, my last connection to Narvik was 7-30am. The sky was blue, the sun was shining; it had snowed but the train was warm, so I went and had a wash to wake me up when I heard we were to be served coffee and rolls! It was a lovely train journey to Narvik, on my arrival at 11am it all seemed very quiet so I went to an office to enquire about the boat I was due to board. To my horror they said the boat was not due to come to Narvik on this voyage, obviously my instructions from the travel agent were incorrect.

The gentleman was helpful and said I would be able to join the boat at Harstad at 7am the following day, and instructed me how to get there by bus, ferry and another bus. I followed the instructions arriving at Harstad at 9pm, feeling very tired. I stayed in a tavern on the dockside overnight, which was rather noisy, and it was a relief the next morning when I boarded the Finnmarken boat, just in time for breakfast!

The fjord steamer had very comfortable cabins, and carried a varied cargo of animals, food, cars, skis, fish, coffins…the lot! Whilst the boat was in port we were able to get off and explore the towns and fishing villages, most had been completely destroyed by the Germans and Russians in the war and a lot of rebuilding had been undertaken.

The boat went to Kirkenes, and we had the option of getting up at 5am to go by bus to the Russian Border, where there was a Norwegian soldier making sure nobody took pictures or used binoculars. At the border there was an area of no man's land and in the distance was a small red house at the Russian border and two flag poles, with one soldier on guard.

Then we passed the River Pasvik, in the distance we could just see a Russian power station, but again no pictures or binoculars were allowed. One of the crew told me that during the war, ten babies were born in the tunnels at Kirkenes. He also told me to notice the age of the children in the villages. They might all be the same age, and with a cheeky smile he told me they must have been born after a bad winter!

The Captain invited everyone to a party, we had a very delicious cream cake and coffee followed by a sing song. The courier Od (his first name) presented our certificates saying we had crossed the Arctic Circle, then he played his accordion and we had an enjoyable evening.

It was very cold and you needed all your clothing on and a blanket round you. I spent an hour or so on the deck the sea was very rough, some of the passengers were sea- sick, but not me!

On our way south we stopped at Hammerfest, which is the northern most town in Europe, it was a glorious day, although we still required warm clothing. Again it was a modern town, the church was typically Norwegian, the pews were painted blue and white, the cross was of mosaic and mainly blue. The shops were interesting and we saw a Lapp woman, they live inland in the winter and move to the coast for the summer. On the return journey to Tromso we went up a cable car to see the midnight sun.

We continued our journey south, the crew pointing out varying sights of interest, the Lofoten Islands with their steep peaks of 4,000 feet, the beautiful Raftsund Channel and the famous Troll fjord, as well as the many different rock formations. The third largest city was Trondheim, founded in 997AD by a Viking King, Olav Trygvason. We had five hours to explore here with the famous 11th century Nidaros Cathedral and the Technical University with 2,000 students.

There were four more stops before we reached Bergen: Kristiansund, Molde with its fine view of 84 snow-capped peaks forming the Romsdal Mountains, Maloy and Floro. An amazing journey that gave me an insight into the life of those who live in these remote areas.

I made my way to the hotel that had been booked for my stay. Bergen is surrounded by seven mountains, a cable car or a funicular railway takes you to the summit of Floyen, where there is a restaurant.

The maternity services were similar in Bergen and Oslo and they both have their own training schools. The larger towns have hospitals and an air service was often used to transport patients from outlying villages. They also had sick hotels, organised by a nursing association, for those requiring frequent treatment or tests needed to reside in the town during that period. They also had homes where unmarried mothers can live for up to six months, until they had time to find suitable accommodation and work.

Norway is a most fascinating country and the people were friendly and hospitable. Their culture is entirely different and attractive, and the people have a love of their national costume and folk museums.

Although I was only in Bergen for five days, my host ensured that I went somewhere special in the evenings. One evening I was taken to see the Finnish National Ballet, they were amazing, the last part - Festivo - was televised. Another evening I was taken by coach to Fana folklore. On the way to Fana church, a Norwegian lady in full national dress spoke about the legends of the trolls, water sprites and other fantasies in Norway. She told us the evening was going to be like a wedding celebration, without a bride. In the church we had an organ recital, a soloist singing, finishing with the wedding march.

The coach then took us up a narrow, steep, winding lane to a cluster of houses. The host was at the gate to greet us, a girl blew on a large cow horn and a fiddler played us up the driveway to a large house, over the door were twigs of juniper and fir, to keep out evil things. There were tables and benches, laid out with crockery, and we all sat down. The fiddler, followed by people in national costume carrying bowls of sour cream porridge, entered the room. Grace was sung by the host, and we were served bowls of porridge, traditional for special occasions, made with semolina, sour cream, and milk, seasoned with a little sugar, with apple juice to drink, it was very delicious. Then smoked mutton was served with thin crisp bread shaped into a figure of eight. The fiddler played and the children danced, then the older ones danced.

After the children left, we were served with coffee and a flat potato cake, spread with butter and sprinkled with sugar. Then the visitors joined in with the dancing and were taught some Norwegian folk songs, causing much fun and laughter. As the sun was going down the fiddler played and we all joined hands as the host sang a song about life. We mounted the coach and waved goodbye, returning to Bergen at 11pm.

My visit to Bergen was over, with grateful thanks to my hosts the Matron of the hospital and her husband, who were both getting on in years, for being so kind and thoughtful.

My final journey by train was to Oslo; the train climbed several thousand feet above sea level, and appreciable amounts of snow lay on the mountains and on the ground. It was a beautiful day, the sun shining brightly on the mountain peaks. As the train descended to a lower level we passed a wide river rushing down with the melting snow from the mountains. At noon I went to the dining car for lunch, for my main course I chose haddock, the fish was so fresh and full of flavour.

On arrival in Oslo I collected my suitcase that I had forwarded from Helsinki, and went to the hotel which had been booked for me, by this time it was early evening and I was tired, so I had an early night to be ready for my last few days.

The following morning I was greeted by a friendly midwife, Else, who took me under her wing for the end part of my three months travelling, I still correspond with Else today. I visited several hospitals and the Oslo Health Centre, which was a hive of activity with a baby clinic and facilities for children up to seven years old, which is the age they start school.

On the ground floor of the clinic was a heated pram shelter, inside they held ante-natal clinics, childcare, relaxation and cookery classes for the mothers. There was a dental department with three surgeries, where children received free treatment, and upstairs was a new family service unit, with specially trained staff to give help and advice to the whole family.

The lives of people feature very much in the history of this fascinating country, and Vigeland Park, Oslo, was an amazing example. In the centre of the park was a tall monolith, surrounded by hundreds of small statues of people of all ages, positioned as though they were struggling for the light. Throughout the park were many other statues depicting scenes in life.

There are many museums in the city - the Viking ship, the Kon Tiki and the Fram museums to name a few. The pride of Oslo must be the City Hall, which was officially inaugurated on 15th May 1950. My host and her husband showed me round. The main entrance had cascades of water and

OSLO

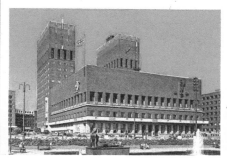

a beautiful swan fountain. All the rooms in the City Hall followed the same theme of life, with large frescoes on the walls, depicting working life in Oslo, in particular the hardships during the war. There was so much to see, it was difficult the take it all in on one visit but the time had come to say goodbye to these lovely, friendly and hospitable people.

On the evening of the 9th June I boarded the ship in Oslo docks, to be greeted by a stewardess who showed me to my cabin. Passengers were given a Welcome Aboard leaflet, giving details about the ship, mealtimes, lifeboat drill, rail connections in England and luggage details.

After a good, calm crossing, there waiting for me in the Newcastle dock yard was Mother, Muriel and Ricky, what a lovely welcome. My luggage was put in the car and we drove home, catching up on the all the news.

On my return home I had to write a report for the scholarship committee and my employers. This was mainly on the technical side of my tour. I filled 21 typewritten foolscap pages with all my visits! Once I had the slides developed, I was asked to give several evening talks to various groups about my hectic three months study tour.

A belated present

Shortly after my return Mother and Muriel had the excitement of a belated Christmas present! On Monday 28th June, I took them to the station to board the boat train to Southampton and begin a nine day cruise on the Reina Del Mar, calling at Vigo, Lisbon and Tangier.

At noon prompt, in Navy style, the order was given to 'up gangway' and we were on our way! We both settled in quickly in our cabin, unpacking our cases and finding our way to the restaurants to ensure we had the first sitting.

S.S. 'REINA DEL MAR' (21,501 TONS)

At 3pm we all had to muster for lifeboat drill, taking our life jackets with us. Whilst all this was happening the pilot had disembarked at the Needles Station and we were heading for the Bay of Biscay. The choice of meals was extensive and very enjoyable. Mother loved the different desserts. Dinner was at 8pm, so after eating we sat in the lounge for a while, then had a walk round the deck, calling for a drink in the Trident lounge, retiring to bed at 10:30 pm feeling very sleepy.

The second day was a lazy day, just enjoying the sun on the deck. The Captain had sent out invitations for cocktails in the Coral Lounge before dinner, later on there was dancing in the lounge.

We were told we would get to Vigo at 8am in the morning, after breakfast we would leave the boat with a guide for a bus tour of Vigo. He told us that sixty years ago Vigo was a small fishing village, but now it was the largest port in Spain and the third largest bay in the world, with a population of 200,000. We passed orange trees growing in the main thoroughfare, and stopped at the Don Castro Park in the grounds of the old palace, which was being restored to be a National Park and Museum.

Vigo Bay is 20 miles long and 10 miles wide and ranked as the third largest in the world, we returned to the boat at 12:30pm and after lunch we spent the afternoon in the sun by the Lido. At 7pm we watched leaving port for the next part of the cruise to take us to Lisbon.

The next morning we were invited to watch 'First Visit to Lisbon', a short, interesting talk and slides for those visiting the city for the first time which we found interesting. Then we went to the sports deck where we had a good view of the River Tagus as the ship wended its way up, docking at 12 noon.

After lunch we decided to go on shore, but after ten minutes of walking agreed that a taxi would be preferable, our driver took us first to the cathedral, where we got out to have a quick look inside, followed by a ride around both old and new Lisbon. The driver told us there had been an earthquake 200 years ago which had destroyed half the city, they rebuilt it with wide avenues, with the scent of beautiful mimosa trees. The taxi took us back to the ship, and had cost us only one pound five shillings.

Vigo

In the evening we joined the 'Lisbon at night' coach trip, which included some Portuguese folksingers and Fados, traditional Portugese songs, performing in a restaurant. The costumes were lovely and the dancing, especially by three men using sticks, was very clever. We returned by a different route, passing an illuminated fountain and arriving back at 1:30am.

After our late night we decided to stay on board playing deck bowls and quoits, Muriel played table tennis with an Irish girl as we sunned ourselves and chatted to other passengers. After lunch we watched the boat leaving Lisbon at 2pm to go to Tangiers, there was a short introduction to the first timers visiting Tangiers.

After dinner we went to the Coral Lounge for the Ocean Derby, where Mother won four shillings in the second race. Then we watched the fancy dress and Ascot hats parade which was very good, about 80 had entered. We retired to bed at 11:30pm.

We awoke to a brilliant morning and land was very quickly coming into sight, we soon docked and by 9:15am were able to go ashore. We talked to

Lisbon

George and Ena from Sunderland who were wondering what to do and I asked if they would like to join us with a taxi, to which they agreed. A guide approached us on the Quayside called Absolum and for £4 he would take us, returning at 12 noon. The ride was simply lovely, beginning with the modern part past various Embassies, then we went into the country we saw camels, goats of various colours, cows and sheep. We stopped to admire 25miles of golden sand, saw the Tuna boats and the Hercules Caves, there were hundreds of large grasshoppers and Cacti all shapes and sizes grew in abundance. We walked through the delightful Palace grounds, through the Kasbah, returning to the gate to rejoin the taxi to take us back for lunch. The rest of the day was spent sun bathing and watching the numerous sellers on the quayside.

At 3am on Sunday 4 July we began our journey back to Southampton, arriving at 7am on 7th July. During the following three days there was a busy programme of activities.

In the high temperatures, sun bathing was high on the list, the children had a fancy dress parade which was very good. There was a Neptune

Tangier

Ceremony when we crossed the equator, which was great fun to watch. Later it was the adults fancy dress parade and gala dance, which we enjoyed watching. On the last day there was a passenger name game, which we were all invited to take part in, followed by the presentation of prizes in the Coral Room and a farewell speech from the Captain.

On the departure day, the Captain, Officers and ship's company of the Reina del Mar wished us happy landings. We said goodbye to our passenger friends and boarded the train to Sheffield, with many happy memories of our cruise.

We had a lovely surprise a few days later when a box containing pink roses arrived from the Union Castle Line; they were beautifully packed in damp straw and tissue paper. It was such a nice box, we kept it and still use it for our Christmas crib scene figures, which just fit in.

Mother and Muriel onboard the Reina Del Mar

The sad news

Following all the excitement, we had to return to normality! The next main event was to prepare for the annual cadet camp which we had already included earlier. Soon after our return from camp, Muriel went through a difficult time, which had begun in 1964 when her boss had a heart attack, and was unable to work for several weeks, so she had to appoint part-time Locums to keep the surgery open. When his condition improved, it was agreed that he should go away for two weeks recuperation; so Muriel drove him and his wife to Conway, North Wales, in their car. A second car accompanied them to bring Muriel home. The Doctor said he should be fine to drive himself back in two weeks, which he was.

All was well until the middle of August 1965 when the dreaded telephone call came, saying he'd had a severe attack from which he did not recover. It became Muriel's job to wind up the practice ready for sale. I was able to use one of the locums from the previous year, who had set up in practice, but not fully booked. There were only a few patients who still required treatment, so this and the necessary forms were done.

It was not necessary to advertise the sale as there was contact with the School of Dentistry at the Dental hospital. One of the newly qualified Dentists was interested and came to view the premises. He asked me if I would stay on as the Dental nurse, but I explained I had been with Mr Fyffe for twenty years and I felt I should have a new beginning as well. He would obviously wish to make alterations and it would be better for him not to have me looking over what he was doing, I think he understood.

16, Hartington Road,
Sheffield 7.

6th. September 1965

<u>TO WHOM IT MAY CONCERN</u>

Miss Muriel Collis has worked for my husband for 20 years. She
came to him as a young girl of 16 years as a trainee Dental Receptionist.
At the outset she proved herself invaluable, she is now a qualified Dental
Nurse, well versed in completing the National Health Service forms and
an excellent Dental Mechanic. I would like to point out that the qualifications
are due entirely to her own efforts.

During the time that Muriel has been with my husband he has not always
been well. She has had complete control of securing a Locum, setting him
to work, completing the necessary forms, arranging appointments and all the
day to day administration.

Finally, I would like to say that Muriel's unfailing happiness, kindness
and consideration made it possible for my husband to continue in the work
he loved until his death.

(Signed) Mrs. Beth Fyffe

Beth Fyffe

Finally, at the end of August I closed the front door for the last time, exactly one month short of twenty years. I wondered what would be waiting on the horizon for me!

This is the end of Part one and Part two in 'Life is What you Make it'; we have only covered thirty six years. As we look back we wonder how we packed everything in! We are continuing our story.

What changes will there be in the seventies and eighties?

Any profit made from the sale of our book will be divided between Village Ventures (Africa) and Hillside Animal Sanctuary, Norfolk.

Dinner! A communal bowl of Maize. Life in Mali, Africa.

Hillside Animal Sanctuary. Rescued Horses enjoying the Hay.